The
INCREDIBLE
FASCINATION
of
VIOLENCE

Dealing with aggression and
brutality among children

Allan Guggenbühl

Translated by Julia Hillman

Spring Publications, Inc.
Woodstock, Connecticut

I would never have learned anything as a child
if I hadn't been beat.

Dr. Samuel Johnson

SPRING PUBLICATIONS, INC.;
299 E. Quassett Road;
Woodstock, Connecticut 06281
http://www.neca.com/ ~ spring

CONTENTS

CHAPTER ONE

FORMS OF VIOLENCE IN SCHOOLS

From outward violence to hidden terror

V iolence among children and teenagers in school is a subject that effects us within. When a nine year old girl suffers in school, has sleepless nights, and over and over again gets beaten up on the playground, we react with sadness or rage. School is supposed to be a place where children flourish and develop. We want to block out the ugly sides of mankind from school and ban them from childhood. Unfortunately experience shows that aggression and violence can break out within school, in the classroom, on the playground, in the hallways or on the way to school, and often dominate the everyday life of a child. This difficult, unpleasant side of mankind does not stop in the world of the child.

If however we compare violence at different schools, it quickly becomes clear that there is no typical form. How violence becomes a problem differs from school to school, classroom to classroom or community to community. Violence presents itself in hundreds of different forms. Depending on how violence shows itself, we have to use different methods to explain it. Forms of violence among children always carry the mark of the school and its children.

We get alarmed the fastest with outward violence. It often shocks us with its brutality and lack of inhibition. This occurs when children torment and beat each other in a way so badly that it clearly has nothing to do with playful rowdiness.

It pleased a class of fifth graders to torment an overweight, visually impaired girl. During recess or on the way to school, a gang of boys, egged on by their classmates, would regularly attack this half invalid girl. They would take her glasses and break them on the ground. Then they would enjoy the helpless fumbling, wandering about and sobbing of the girl. This girl's visual impairment became the cause for a macabre game.

Violence happens not only to individuals who stand out, but can also effect entire groups. In a Zürich school, "dwarf throwing" became popular. This was a competition where, during recess, fifth and sixth graders would grab the first graders and line them up in a field. Then the older students would see who could throw a little boy or girl the farthest in the field.

Violence in the form of hidden terror between different age groups occured in a school in Bern. Right next to the school there was a record store. The owner complained to the school about the frequent theft of compact discs. It came to his attention that especially small children were stealing CD's. The elementary school teachers reacted in disbelief and indignation. It was impossible for them to imagine that their first and second graders would set out on thieving missions. They thought there was a misunderstanding and denied the possibility of the accusations. During our crisis intervention, where we also work with the students, it came out that the school was being terrorized by a group of sixth grade boys. These older students ordered the younger ones to steal CD's, otherwise they would be beaten. The elementary students kept quiet because they feared the older students' retaliation. Neither parents nor teachers heard about it.

Besides outward verbal violence, there are hidden forms of violence difficult to recognize, that unfortunately, mostly stay concealed from the teacher. In a classroom, we noticed how students would squeeze their way along the windows in order to reach the teacher's desk. The wider, middle isle would not be used. The teacher explained this behavior (to herself) as a "fashion." Through the crisis intervention, it came to light that it bothered a group in the class when their classmates used the middle isle. They therefore gave the order to use the isles by the windows. The student who did not conform had to count on retaliation during recess. To the students it was clear who was giving the orders in this class. The teacher was regarded as rather insignificant.

Often violence gets settled verbally. For example, obscene insults are common in school. And where the crudest language is used, fecal or sexual words are thrown around in groups of children. In such cases, language serves as a weapon to hurt others.

The escalation of verbal violence can also be seen in writing. In an essay, a boy imagines how a classmate, Karin, should be treated.

> First she was hanged, then her arms and legs were ripped off. Then her tongue was ripped out, and her stomach split open. Then a bomb was placed in her mouth and Karin exploded. The end.

Whether violence appears directly or in a hidden form, it affects us and challenges us to take action, especially now when children are tormented in school, and the disputes on the playground are no longer harmless brawls. Teachers, psychologists and parents cannot passively watch children suffer, so we have to think about what can be done about violence and aggression among children.

The power of the gang

As a child psychologist, you notice over and over again, that children who, according to teacher and parent descriptions, are supposed to be delinquents and particularly aggressive, seem harmless on a one-on-one basis. A boy who was feared by the entire school as a tough sits peacefully across from me and says solemnly with wide-open eyes that he is opposed to violence. Convincingly, he claims that conflicts should be resolved in discussion and not through violence. He might even complain about other children who act in an aggressive and rude way on the playground. He does not consider himself one of them, however. As a psychologist, you encounter over and over again the phenomenon of the so called bad or aggressive child who acts peacefully face-to-face. Their verbal statements regarding conflicts, violence, and fights do not differ greatly from those of the teaching staff. They swear they reject violence. Unfortunately I have often observed how these nice resolutions go up in smoke as soon as these boys and girls are among their peers. When these children or teenagers are among themselves, a different kind of reality takes over. The attractive blond boy who complains about his aggressive classmates can five minutes later run towards a group of girls with a raised fist, shouting, "Can you smell death in the air?" His earlier principles are forgotten. He does not see a contradiction in his behavior. He is not violent, but the girls gave him a "stupid look."

This strange change in behavior is explained by the gang or group phenomenon. If children or teenagers are among themselves, a different reality takes hold of them. The standards of personal behavior lose their validity. The group decides how to behave. What the children do, say and strive for is influenced by the dynamics of the group. They feel that they are in another world. Good boys and girls turn into wild warriors. The timid girl changes into a fresh brat. The children feel part of a gang. They are no longer merely an individual related to a mother or father, teacher or friend. They are a member of a group and experience the community of people their age.

In this group, children produce a counter world. It has to be clearly different from the adult world. The children notice that they are in a different world where they are in command. Adults cannot push them around there. In the group the children feel that they can seize the world.

The group or gang feeling expresses itself through different characteristics. One characteristic is the language of the children. Children choose words that distinguish themselves from adult language. There is talk using words like "horny," "super-horny," "check it out," or "super-cool." Often words are chosen that give the children the feeling of power or expressions that provoke a reaction from adults. The children need this jargon, because it confirms their feeling of empowerment. If the teacher, father or mother are appalled, it proves their power. The blushing of the teacher when obscene expressions are used, confirms the group's feeling. Nothing is more annoying than when a teacher reacts with understanding. Children often get irritated when a teacher empathetically tells a child that she or he can well understand why the child is using obscene expressions, or when a teacher tries to make the expressions harmless or tries to explain away their meaning. The effect is lost when the teacher does not get upset but instead is objective. Then one's power cannot be celebrated.

In one class, it was observed how the use of these obscene and aggressive words escalated because the teacher did not react. Finally the students started greeting one another with the "Hitler" salute. The ideology of the extreme right was alien to these boys and girls, but they felt that through these words and action, they provoked a reaction in the teacher. Her sheer horror was a relief to them. At last, they were seen as a group with power.

Gang or group behavior is also expressed through clothing. In many schools there are actual, although unstated, dress codes. The children orient themselves on their peer groups' uniforms. In certain schools the group decides that only one brand of sneakers is to be worn. Often not only the brand is prescribed, but also how they should be worn, "untied with the tongue hanging out." There are ways that t-shirts and baseball caps are to be worn. In individual schools and communities in Zürich, there are certain rules as to where football jackets can be worn. The "Raider" jacket, for example, is reserved for the students of the eastern Zürich lake shore.

In one school it became obvious that students were starting to wear pants up to four sizes too big for them. Since the children picked out their own clothes, the parents could do nothing about it. These oversized pants were then worn backwards with the zipper in the back.

In another school it was observed how the first and second graders wore their jackets with their shoulders free. The mothers who accompanied them to school kept on pulling up the shoulders of the jackets, but as soon as the children were alone, they pulled the jackets back down to expose their shoulders. By wearing the jackets in this fashion, the children signaled that they had distanced themselves from adults and lived in their own world.

In a group or gang, children can experience the feeling of greatness. They can have the feeling of being in a group that is noticed and from which one has to be careful. The consequences of these inflated feelings are that individual actions often are largely overestimated. For example, two ten year old boys mentioned casually to me on their way out of school, that together, after their visit with me, they were going to raise hell in the town. All of Bern marvels when they cruise through the old city.

The gangs can actually exist in reality, but sometimes they are only fantasized. Then the children imagine themselves as part of a larger community, while in reality no gang exists. Smaller children imagine themselves as Ninja Turtles—"Raphaelo" or "He-Man." Later they see themselves as a "homie" or a ninja fighter, even if they are the only member of the gang. If there are two or three of them, the children believe to be part of a movement. These children orient themselves internally on the notion that they belong to a gang and act accordingly. Such small gangs often look for their idols in the video or music scene. They try to go down the hallway like a rock star or to dress like a movie star. Particularly introverted children seek, through their imagination, to connect to group idols to feel empowered.

Group experiences are important for psychological reasons. In the gang or group, children are confronted with realities of human existence which cannot be conveyed in a school curriculum. In groups, children encounter existential challenges that we also battle with in adult life: betrayal, intrigues, overcoming fear, feuds, quarrels and jealousy. They are faced with the ugly sides of mankind but also learn to mobilize capabilities in order to deal with these dark forces. They discover the meaning of friendship, loyalty, of contracts or experience how fights are settled. In the group a spontaneous social learning takes place. Contents are conveyed that could never be packaged into a school class.

An older woman told how, during her childhood in her group, actual trials were staged. If a boy assaulted another child, or if he went too far in a fight, a tribunal was held in the forest. A trial was held, and it was decided what would be tolerated and what would be punished. The children created these trials themselves.

In these child subworlds, children encounter the negative sides of mankind but also acquire social skills. The subworlds start to fall apart once the children get older. Often discrepancies within a student body become apparent in the seventh to ninth grades. The collective world crumbles and individuals come out: there are skate boarders, computer freaks and mountain-bikers. In girls different tendencies also become apparent: the socially engaged versus aerobic enthusiasts or disco freaks versus the ones who love to read. At this age common guidelines are rarer. Therefore this age group often feels disoriented. The group feeling of childhood is gone and gives way to an adjustment to a subgroup norm.

In school there then is the danger that if an ideal is lacking, a psychologically obscure situation is created. Teenagers who are neglected, socially damaged, or slightly uninhibited, take over power. They steer the direction of the group when no common ideas pervade.

A high school in the northern part of Zürich was completely taken in by the sparkling personality of a classmate. This girl of mixed race cast a spell over her fellow students through her self confidence, her looks and lack of inhibitions. The entire class followed her. For her girl friends, she would at times seduce men in a shopping center of the town. She convinced a male classmate to commit burglary and theft. She drove her teacher to desperation because she attended class only when she liked. Together with a boy and a girlfriend, she controlled the entire class. If any of the three were criticized, she would have a group of friends storm into the hallways. Such a scene worked. Nobody dared criticize any of the three friends. The problem in this situation was that the tone was set by a subgroup that was not actually representative of the group.

Street boys: an historical retrospective

Naturally gangs are nothing new for children. Children have always been initiated into the realities of human existence through their gangs or groups. In the previous centuries, "street boys" annoyed citizens and made villages and towns unsafe.

> In the towns, the street boys ruled. . . in an almost intolerable manner. Every game turned into trouble. Not only did their whips crack around the good citizens' ears, but often enough they also hit him or her with a good swing. You had to avoid their iron barrel hoops otherwise you would get them between your legs, trip, and fall miserably to the ground with their shouting at you. Many a respectful lady felt, with horror, one of these hoops roll up against her dress. It was an everyday event for the sly rascals to shoot darts and clay bullets with a crossbow, toy bow or blowpipe at innocent maidens or girl servants. Spinning tops, the small one as well as the humming one, seem to have been invented only to make walking miserable for people on the wide avenues where the ground already was unsafe by the infamous nine marbles present every ten steps. If an absent-minded pedestrian did not pay attention to the spinning tops, the boys would

treat his legs like their toy and whip into them. If you happened to break it by stepping on it, there was an unavoidable silent petition for a new one. If a street boy did not have a spinning top, he amused himself by throwing stones, clods of dirt, and really enjoyed harassing carriages. No horse remained untormented, no stagecoach was safe. To be able to cross the street in front of a wagon was considered quite an achievement. If the coachman pulled back on the horses so they would rear up, and people would yell, "The unfortunate child is under the wheels," then the rough boy and his friends would laugh with scorn. It was not the sons of the poor who made use of the newly imported firecrackers and rockets from East India causing nights of unholy mischief on the streets. They would throw showers of sparks into the midst of an unsuspecting crowd . . . or in between the horses of a coach so the horses would break away. Or they would throw them into the stagecoaches full of fancy ladies and gentlemen. Whigs, toupees, crinolines, and velvet coats would burn or be completely ruined from the fireworks. Then the godless horde of boys would shout with joy, split up, run and disappear into lanes and cross alleys.[1]

These descriptions of the street boys in Hamburg in 1741 show that gang activity among children is nothing new. Children have always partially oriented themselves in their behavior after their peers. Apart from the crowded apartment, the workshop, and the classroom, much of a child's life was played out on the streets. Often gangs of children would get so bad, the authorities had to step in. On 4 May 1765 it was declared:

---

[1] Katharina Rutschky, *A German Children's Chronicle* (Cologne: Kiepenheuer & Witsch, 1983), 361.

After hitherto displeasingly having experience that all
warnings by the teachers did not suffice in stopping
the young's mischievousness in graveyards, streets,
embankments, and on the avenues, we therefore deem
it necessary to give support by order of the authorities, to the teachers' well meaning efforts: in this way
parents, guardians, and all those to whom the care
over children is their duty that are with them, are to
be reminded once again to urge their children to a
Christian respectable behavior, also outside of their
houses and to, in no way, allow them to play and
throw things or produce other kinds of mischief in the
graveyards, streets or other aforesaid public places . . .
So, negligent parents and guardians are to be warned
that orders have been given that young people who
carry on mischief in the graveyards, on the streets, and
in other public places will be arrested, and according
to what is deemed necessary by the authorities, will be
publicly punished in the town hall square, whereby
the parents, guardians, and others who have the children in their care will be absolutely held legally and
financially responsible for all damages caused by their
mischievous children.

Göttingen, 4 May 1765[2]

School as gang territory

Gangs are nothing new. The children gang's place of
action, however, has relocated. While in earlier days, the
children's groups gathered primarily outside of school,
children today seek gang experiences inside school. Gangs
are no longer active in the streets, and one's age group is
no longer celebrated in the woods, churchyards, gardens
or abandoned factory buildings. The school, the classroom, and the playground serve as the place for gang or
group life. Schools today are confronted with the

---

[2] Ibid., 226-27.

challenges of violence and aggression because of this shift.

Different reasons led to this shifting of territories. First, the dangerous way to school now poses greater challenges to children. The dangers of traffic make it necessary for us to insist that our children behave in the street. They must walk on the sidewalk, wait in front of the crossings, are never allowed to cross the streets with a red light, and have to look to their right and left before crossing a street. Thanks to the teaching of street rules to our children, the risks of accidents have decreased. Most school children can comprehend the dangers of traffic and act accordingly. Children adapt to the adult's and police's demands, because they have no interest in being run over. They behave more or less well on their way to school, as the way to school demands they adapt.

Unfortunately this demand also has a disadvantageous side effect. The undisciplined, half chaotic atmosphere of going to school has disappeared. Roaming about, dawdling, running around, wrestling and doing pranks are not possible. The field of exploration in going to school is lost. Children go home directly or are picked up by their parents. They have less time to meet up and bond with other children. Gangs rarely become active on the way to school. If a child marches out of school wearing an orange traffic strip knowing that he or she has to be home in ten minutes, the chance of a gang coming together is not possible.

A further reason for the shifting of the place of action of the gangs lies in the humanization of schools. Up until a couple of decades ago, schools were considered institutions that children feared. For the majority of children however, school was, if at all frequented, a place of training, of sitting still, of thrashings and of rote learning. Students could never know how a teacher was going to react. You had to be prepared for punishment, expulsion, or to be a victim of a teacher's mood. From a child's perspective, schools often were institutions of horror that instilled respect through punishment and their arbitrariness. Schools and teachers were feared. You tried to get out of them as quickly as possible.

Today, schools have become more humane. This has the undisputed advantage that children feel more comfortable there. They fear the teachers less. They are not impressed with them as figures of terror, and teachers show a sympathy for children. In the classroom the consequences can be that the teacher is no longer experienced as a dominant figure but as a member of the group.

A fifth grade teacher complained to the parents about their daughter's dirty, lewd behavior. According to the teacher, the girl would routinely slap the teacher's behind. The teacher found this unmannerly and wondered about the girl's impertinence.

It is a sign of progress that schools have become more humane, that children today can develop more freely and be themselves in school. But unfortunately the desire for gang activity is also acted out in school, and specific group dynamics show up in the realm of the classroom. Where previously children adjusted to the teacher, peer group activities are now the center of their attention. In the schools of Bern, surveys show that for children events in their own group are of much greater interest than learning or the teacher.

Finally the shifting of gang territory is related to the number of children in our society. The presence of children in our society has gone down because the number of children per family has decreased, the population's adults are on the increase, and the available living space per person has increased. On the streets, in the stores, and in public places, children are clearly in the minority. The leisurely rhythm of quieter adults dominates and not the sound of hollering children or the running around of girls and boys. Children have pulled back from public life, since they cannot hold their own faced with the superior number of adults. Children are only permitted to be in designated areas like playgrounds. Yet because these are closely watched over by mothers, it is also unlikely that gangs will form there. Playgrounds are territories especially designed for children, so this is another reason why it is not a place where children can seize the world. Children are supposed to swing back and forth on swings, crawl down pipes or slide down ropes. They indulge such activities with pleasure, but the appropriation of the outside world through gangs does not take place. The mysterious, overpowering and inexplicable, what children perceive as the outside world, is blocked out. To play in a sandbox you do not need a gang.

The over-teaching of children

The last reason for the shift of gang and group activities of children into schools is what I call over-teaching. This occurs in the extensive demands on children through organized recreation or other activities. The weekly schedules of children are full. Besides school, they are engaged in many activities: karate classes on Monday, expressive painting on Tuesday, the pony group on Wednesday afternoon, English for early starters on Friday, and Boy or Girl Scouts on Saturday. Children have almost no free time. Taken separately, these efforts are meaningful and are usually received with excitement by the children, but there is a danger of going overboard. Their lives are too planned because of the attempt to always stimulate children. Yet most children seek out these activities. They want to draw, paint, play with dough, exercise or even learn foreign vocabularies, but in this way boredom is also avoided. The monotony of an endless free afternoon is necessary so children can develop ideas. If children are seduced by programs, they hardly ever experience boredom. They try to meet an instructor's expectations and miss out on the fascination and the monotony of roaming around in a group. Today, there are fewer possibilities for children to form into gangs because they are too busy.

The humanizing of the schools, the reduction of the number of children, and over-teaching are reasons why children look for their microcosmos in schools today. As stated earlier, through gangs children are confronted with a part of life's reality. Through them they experience the positive as well as the negative sides of human existence. The shifting of the gang's place of activity is a reason why the image of violence has changed. Today violence often occurs in schools because less opportunities for it are present outside of school. Now the demon of violence has chosen school as the place to play.

CHAPTER TWO

THE JUNGLE GENERATION

Homeboys or the desire for a personal myth

P sychologically speaking, a gang, or just a group of children, does not live in a vacuum. Youth groups need a collective fantasy with which to identify; a collective scenario that offers them the possibility in which to imagine themselves. On the one hand, it has to capture the qualities of their existence, and on the other, it needs to be clearly different from the adult world as seen by the children. This collective scenario represents a subculture, and in it a counter-world is described that is shunned by adults. This scenario contains images and symbols that express a personal life sense (or, in other words, a myth) that lets each generation and time feel unique.

Every gang or group of children searches for a myth through which they are guaranteed a personal history. Since no generation wants to enter into a society quietly and unnoticed, each generation searches for a feeling of uniqueness, its own origins or roots. These origins are called upon when various problems and challenges arise. They provide the reason for one's actions, and they give young people an entrance into the world. This origin myth is the story that unbuttons a child from a purely personal existence and gives life a sense of meaning.

Young people glean the myths or collective scenarios from information available to them. Often it is images from the media—especially the music and film industry—that offer children a wide spectrum of possible figures and scenarios with which to identify. The multimedia network of the Western World has given its children images from an array of subcultures. They hear of the street life of children in Rio de Janeiro. They see pictures of young people in Jamaica that, along with Reggae, give meaning to their life. They also know what is happening in New York, London, Paris and other cities. Through the media, children are presented with different worlds in which they can mirror themselves. Out of this immense amount of images and symbols, every few years a new myth is constellated. Every generation seems to choose a subculture that becomes the carrier of their sense of meaning.

If we look at the collective scenarios of the past three generations, we see that in each instance a different part of the world becomes the carrier of a myth. The existentialists of the 50's elected Paris as their Mecca. Paris radiated a life attitude that rejected every faith and every value. For a short time in the 60's, London became the carrier of a myth: one simultaneously identified a new sense of meaning with rock-and-roll which was spread by *The Beatles*, *The Rolling Stones* and others. Everything was happening in London. Later San Francisco took over this role with Flowerpower. *It* was happening on Haight-Ashbury in San Francisco. Thousands of this generation imagined themselves in California and imitated the subculture. In the eyes of their generation, new values and attitudes towards life were born. The subculture helped along its own narrative.

Today's collective scenario or myth is that of ghetto kids. The myth of the homeboy became huge at the end of the 80's and the beginning of the 90's. Thousands of children pattern themselves on the fantasies they project onto gangs in the streets of New York, Chicago, and Los Angeles. They see themselves as jungle fighters who have to prove themselves in a complex, hostile world. The homeboy myth serves as the collective fantasy for today's generation.

As with every myth, it is of course possible to interpret in different ways. A myth is not a concrete explanation but a psychological scenario that captures a sense of life. Certain children emphasize music. For them *rap* is what is important.

For other children and teenagers rap isn't important. Break dancing or hip-hop are. These dance forms, which were for the most part developed by black American children in the big cities, are copied. Thanks to these unique forms of dance, many children succeed in finding new ways to move. For a third group, graffiti is the most important. They spray designs and tags[1] on concrete walls. So the homeboy mythos has different facets. According to one's preference, different aspects are emphasized.

Besides these qualities of the homeboy mythos which often have a creative effect on the everyday life of children and teenagers, there unfortunately can be a destructive interpretation. Whereas violence was taboo in the hippie movement, it is partly sought out and celebrated in the homeboy mythos. Violence is not rejected but looked to as a possibility to bring oneself into being. The homeboy mythos also evokes the image of the street

---

[1] Editor's note: These are names that mark their territories.

fighter who defends himself with a baseball bat, ninja star or brass knuckles. In the image that many young people have of homeboys, violence is a possibility of finding meaning. Homeboys do not actually have to be more violent than other youth groups, but in their myth, violence is allowed.

In individual homeboy groups (in Switzerland), this shows itself through the particular rituals of violence that kids carry out. Children make a distinction between the *toys* and the real homeboys. Eleven to thirteen year olds belong to the *toys*. In order to be accepted by the older homeboys they must beat up an asylum-seeker or homosexual. Only after having committed such a violent act are they acknowledged as a homeboy.

Here are words of a home boy from Los Angeles.[2]

> I'm tryin' to do is make a name for myself. I tryin' to have a bad rep—I got a little reputation, but it ain't nearly where I want it to be. I want to be known. I want to be criminal, mean or both. I want to fulfill my name. Be a straight criminal, be devious, do anything, be bad to the fullest. You know what I'm talkin' about? Anybody want to fight, we can fight. Anybody want to shoot, we can shoot. Want to kill, we can kill. *Whatever*.

Homeboys see things differently from their perspective. It is not they who are violent but the other gang or the police. Often they think in distinct friend-enemy terms which allows aggressive actions to be taken against members of other gangs or the law. When asked why they kill, the homeboys in correction centers of California answer, "Cause he's my enemy."[3]

---

[2] Léon Bing, *Do or Die* (New York: HarperCollins, 1991), 20-21.
[3] Ibid., 121.

From the perspective of these groups, exterior things or insignificant grounds are viewed as legitimate reasons for violence. The harassment of one's fly-girl by another gang, the wearing of the L.A. Raider jacket in the wrong territory or the wrong brand of sneakers, demand retaliation. From the point of view of the gangs, these are bold actions that have to be punished with force. Gang members of the Crips and Bloods in Los Angeles therefore accuse each other of senseless brutality. Their own actions are legitimized because the other side is viewed as even worse.

Here is a statement of an ex-Blood from South Central Los Angeles.[4]

> I been a Crips since I was thirteen years old, I'm true blue, but them kids are scandalous. How about a two-year-old baby blasted outta her mama's arms 'cause she wearin' red shoelaces?! The *baby* wearin' red shoelaces! These kids just shoot anybody.

Only a small percentage of Swiss children and teenagers act out violence the way certain homeboy groups in the United States do. As mentioned, the myth of ghetto kids is richly faceted. In the homeboy mythos, violence is partially legitimized within the context of fighting for survival in the jungle.

Violence as a cry for help

I have tried to show the importance that the group or gang has for children. I have described how fights within one's age group and *outsider* gangs have moved into Swiss schools. Further we have looked at the collective fantasies or myths on which the children or teenager groups base themselves. Only a part of the violence in schools is done

---

[4] Ibid., 105.

by such gangs. Every teacher will confirm that violent actions in schools cannot all be linked to secret gang wars. Often certain aggressive, uninhibited children stand out as culprits. These children are often damaged by their environment and beaten up at home, venting their subsequent frustration at school. These students become violent out of mental despair. Their violence is a cry for help. Often they are children who have not integrated well socially. They feel that they are aliens, victims, or outsiders. Their heightened aggression is a desperate attempt to gain acceptance in their age group. There isn't a gang behind their behavior but rather personal problems: Giovanni is a fifth grader and lives in a suburb of Bern. He is shunned by his classmates. They accuse him of being brutal. He hits boys in the stomach, pulls girls by the hair and bites his opponents. Everything that Giovanni does and says is rejected by the others.

On a one on one basis, Giovanni is talkative and accessible. He proudly tells of his father's connection with the Sicilian Mafia and that he comes from a terrific Italian family. Moreover he fantasizes about the great soccer team that he will soon found. What is noticeable is the great difference between the perception of himself and the description of him by his classmates. While he imagines himself as a big-shot, he is in fact an outsider.

During counseling it became clear that Giovanni is beaten by his father on a regular basis. His mother is resigned, apathetic and seems to have given up internally. Giovanni is fleeing to these inflated fantasies in order to preserve his feeling of worth. His aggressiveness must be seen in connection with his inner distress.

When violence and aggression in school classes come from these particular difficult students, they need individual psychological care. Their appeals must be taken seriously.

However, there is another viewpoint from a group psychological perspective. Whether these difficult, uninhibited or environmentally damaged children persist in being problematic or whether their tendencies are neutralized by the group depends on the rest of the children, on the makeup of the school class, its atmosphere, on the collective fantasies and internal groupings. There is a greater chance that the problem children will set the tone in groups of children with a weak structure. If, however, the children as a group have developed checks that can be put up against the demands of the problem children, the chances of avoiding brutal violence are better. The positive group forces reduce the influence of the aggressive children.

Rituals against violence

Rituals are the positive side of a gang or children's group. A ritual is a stereotypic behavior that is used under certain challenges. Rituals are a collective series of patterned actions that are there to help master difficult situations, when dangers threaten, and in transitions like marriage, birth or death. Rituals come into play in order to give security as well as to prevent brutal urges from taking over. Rituals are always group related. From ethnology we know of different ritual forms that are used by people or tribes when dealing with violence.

The landscape of Papua New Guinea, the great half-island state bordering on Indonesia, is marked by mountains and forests. In the different valleys live tribes that have their own languages. Many of these tribes are at war with each other. The wars often last for months and take up an enormous amount of energy and time. What is striking is that even with all these war activities, there are relatively few dead or injured. A tribe may dress in a war-like fashion, paint themselves and angrily charge the enemy without actually being destructive and deadly.

If one takes a closer look at these war campaigns, certain patterns are recognizable. One tribe charges towards the other with loud shouts. The other falls back in order to regroup and then charges back shouting. In between, spears fly. Each tribe indulges in boasting which consists of exaggerated descriptions of their own capabilities and wealth. The opposite tribe is given a humiliating tirade of insults and is described as pitiful. There is a generous amount of bragging and insulting. Often, as proof of personal wealth, a cow, dragged from the village, pays the price. It is slaughtered on the open field so that the other tribesmen can see their competitor's wealth. Naturally the other tribe has to then get even and also sacrifice one or two cows. This form of ritual warfare—which unfortunately now only sometimes happens in Papua New Guinea—was a pain in the neck for the resident Australian aid workers. This warfare kept on destroying their efforts to build up the agriculture of Papua New Guinea. Cows given to the tribes kept ending up dead on the battlefield.

Similar ritual forms of violence can be observed in different tribes of Asia, Africa, and South America. These rituals allow for token violence so that tensions are released without resulting in death or destruction. The ritual curbs the aggression by embedding it into a social form.

Interestingly, similar rituals can be seen among school children. Under favorable conditions, behavioral patterns develop in which children can act out their aggressions. A little violence flickers up without being brutally expressed.

It was customary in a fourth grade class that every Friday someone got beaten up. In the morning the victim's name would be announced. For example, "It is going to be Bärbel's turn this afternoon!" It was clear that the beatings would take place at the end of the last afternoon class. Accordingly the tension grew steadily during the day. The school children feverishly awaited for the event, stood by the victim, were afraid themselves or joined the attackers. However what was remarkable with this class was that it rarely ever turned into a brawl. Since the victim was already known in the morning, he or she could take the necessary precautions. After the last class, the chosen victim could run home as fast as possible not to be caught. Rarely or never did it occur that the victim was actually captured and beaten. In this class violence was ritualized.

There are many examples of gang wars between children and teenagers from different villages. A father tells how during his school days, they (as boys from Witikon, a section of Zürich) would prepare themselves for confrontations with the mean boys of Zollikon (a village next to the city). Throughout their school years they would forge plans and try to find out what the mean boys on the other side of the hill were up to. There would be talk about the upcoming big battle, the day of reckoning. Personally he and his cohorts never got to see these mean Zolliker boys face to face, and to this day he is not certain whether these Zolliker boys actually existed.

Similar ritual forms of fighting exist between different city quarters in Switzerland. The Wipkinger boys (a district of Zürich) were constantly preparing themselves for war against the Obersträssler boys (a different city district). The two groups would meet on a particular field from time to time. Contrary to the Zolliker boys, the Obersträsslers would often actually show up, make threatening gestures, and throw rocks at the Wipkinger boys. Preparations and threats were repeatedly made whereas actual fighting was rare.

Rituals can become a tradition. In Brunnen, in the canton of Schwyz, at Christmas time St. Nicholas was portrayed with two attendants. Called "Mutzlis," two boys from the village were chosen to portray them. When St. Nicholas passed through the town, the boys, who were dressed in brown cowls, were allowed to beat up anyone they happened to meet.

A colleague told me how a particular game established itself at his boarding school during his school days. If a fellow student broke any rule of the group, he would be forced to play a punishment game. With only a pillow held by two of its corners for defense, he had to stand on a bed, and the other boys would face him. When the referee, an older student, blew the whistle, the other boys started beating him. The game was only allowed to take place on the bed, and the older student decided when the game was over.

Such rituals of violence that prevent worse from happening are often observed in the school recess area. Fighting goes on, but it is agreed that as soon as one of the fighters is down on the ground, the fight is over. Fights are equal and biting, scratching, hair pulling, and strangling are not allowed.

Rituals developed by cohesive groups are the only answer to impending violence. By permitting a small amount of violence they prevent it from getting out of control. Such rituals must be developed and carried out by children themselves. It is an illusion to believe that we can ban violence and aggression from the world of the child. Violence will always be there, but the idea is to find a social form that excludes destructive, brutal, and uninhibited violence. The tendency towards violence seems to be a basic human instinct. To want to ban it is useless. To do so would merely shift the acts of violence or even escalate them. Violence can only be managed with the help of positive reinforcement in children's groups, and rituals are a valuable way to curb the violent tendencies in children.

Previously, Zürich had a ritual form of violence that worked well. This was called the school Silvester. On the last day of the school year, the children would get up at four or five in the morning, take lids from pots and pans, horns, bells and other noise makers, and go through the streets waking the good citizens out of their sleep. The idea was to disturb the adult world. The ringing of door bells was very popular. If one could get somebody out of their bed and to the door, the prank was a success. The highest achievement of one's efforts was to see an adult's furious face. Besides the noise and the waking up of the neighbors, pranks were a part of the school Silvester. With pleasure, garden gates were unhinged, cars covered with shaving cream, or garden furniture hidden. There was a whole range of actions that, although forbidden, were done anyway and without actually being destructive.

At the end of the 60's, teachers, school administrators and concerned parents tried to curb the goings on of the school Silvester. The indoor swimming pools were opened early in the morning and the teachers were urged to lure the children into the schools with an attractive, alternative morning program. Furthermore people were advised to disconnect their doorbells. The police imposed a curfew that did not allow anyone to pass through the streets before six o'clock in the morning.

In fact many children streamed into school and joined in on hikes and disco parties. Many parents and teachers thought that the children were now away from the streets and not involved in any mischief.

Unfortunately the effect was to the contrary. The good, well adjusted children did go to school. Many however decided to get up even earlier and did even more violent activities. Since the ritual was destroyed through a concerted educational effort, mail boxes were now blown up, cars scratched, windshields shattered and garbage cans set on fire. Without the ritual, violence appeared in a raw and destructive form. The well intentioned educational efforts caused the opposite effect. It destroyed a ritual that had developed over decades within the world of children as an attempt to curb their own violent tendencies.

Violence in the media

One subject that preoccupies minds over and over again is violence in the media. In the news, in movies or on video tapes, children are presented with violent images. Whether in *Rambo*, *The Class of 84*, or in the actual reports of assaults, violence is omnipresent in the media. Daily we can watch murder, hold ups, fights and acts of destruction on our TV screen. Early on, children are confronted with these horrific scenes. In addition there are different computer games where people are shot down, airplanes exploded and even atomic wars staged. Such games alarm us. We find it repulsive that such horrible incidents on TV should serve as an outlet for our play instinct. Don't video games, the media and movies have a brutalizing influence on children?

The media's and video games' effect are under intense discussion. Studies seem to suggest that violent scenes on TV increase the readiness for aggression. In fact, however, these studies only prove that there is an increase in the state of excitement and the tendency to play war games.

That children actually do become more violent and uninhibited in their every day life is not proven.[5] To the question of the influence of the media, there is the following to be said:

The deciding factor is how the children react to violent scenes, what the incident "does" with the child, and what psychological processes are released. It is too simple to assume that the child will imitate exactly the scene from television or videos. If simply presenting examples were as effective as that, our schools would be a gigantic success. Children's reactions to images on television are complex. An exact acting out is only one of many possible ways of reacting.

Another known way to react is to set up a defense: the violent scene is so horrific, the child does not want to perceive it. It closes it's eyes, focuses on the good in the movie, and overlooks the violence. This is how a child protects itself. Many children react in this way. The horrible is not registered.

A further way of reacting is fictionalization: when watching a violent scene, these children ask themselves whether or not it is reality or fiction. If a movie is seen as fiction, it allows them to watch it without damage to the psyche. What takes place in front of their eyes is a form of a fairy tale. It is a terrifying story that brings fear and delight but has nothing to do with reality. From the start children have a finely tuned sensibility for fictitious

---

[5] Huesmann, L. R., Mammuth, N. M., "Media Violence and Antisocial Behaviour," *Journal of Social Issues,* 1986, vol. 42, No. 3.

scenes.[6] They know how to differentiate what is true and what is specially created for the movies. Most violent movie scenes are categorized as staged violence. As a rule such scenes do not have an uninhibiting effect on the children but possibly lead to a slightly heightened state of excitement.

Another way of reacting is that of disgust. Many children mobilize moral categories when watching violent scenes. They get outraged, are shocked and supported in their rejection of violence. With this kind of reaction it is not the violent tendencies but the rejection thereof that is being reinforced. The movie sensitizes them to a subject that is also of their concern and one they must learn to master.

Finally there is imitation. Here children look for models in the movies. They mimic what they see. For example, three third grade boys dragged a girl to their home. Their parents were not in. They tied her to the bed and pretended that "they were going to fuck her." The children did not know what " fucking" really meant. Without taking their clothes off, they tried to lay on top of the girl and make jerky movements. Evidently points were given in a video game for this kind of behavior. In this terrible incident, where the boys staged a rape without actually executing a sexual act, imitation was at the forefront. They wanted to reenact a scene that they had seen on a video game. The game had a brutalizing effect on these boys. Children let themselves be influenced by videos and violent scenes in the media. However the question is whether these horrible scenes really always encourage brutality and violence. Do the children learn violent behavior through these videos or do they merely

---

[6] Theunert et al., *Zwischen Vergnügen und Angst—Fernsehen im Alltag von Kindern* (Berlin: Vistas-Verlag, 1992).

use these images to vent their already existing violent tendencies?

Three boys in the third grade kidnapped a girl from their class one Wednesday afternoon.[7] They dragged her into a shed and locked her into a rabbit cage. Then they announced to her that she was about to be hanged. They shoved to her a piece of dry bread and sprinkled her with water announcing that this was to be her last meal. In front of the totally frightened girl they tied a rope around a beam and told her to prepare herself for her last hour.

Although the boys finally abandoned their scheme, this experience was highly unpleasant for the girl. When asked later where they got the idea to hang one of their school mates, they replied, embarrassed, "In Sunday school!" The Sunday school teacher had told the children a story about someone who gets tied to a stake and then hanged as punishment. From that story, the boys came to the conclusion that unpopular contemporaries are to be punished in this way, although that certainly was not the intention of the Sunday school teacher. Since this girl fit into the category of being unpopular (according to the boys), they decided to take action.

A closer look at the personal history of these boys shows that they already had a tendency towards violence. In kindergarten the leader of this group stood out because of his brutal behavior towards his class mates. He once hit a girl so severely over the head with his jacket that she ran home screaming and refused to go back to kindergarten that day.

This is just one example to show how the media doesn't have a one sided effect on children, and that the cause of violence doesn't come only from the brutalizing

---

[7] Editor's note: In Switzerland school children are free every Wednesday afternoon but go to school on Saturday mornings.

influence of violent videos. Many children choose violent role models out of a certain tendency and lust for violence. An aggressive potential searches for a figure through whom a child can express itself. The decisive factor is *how* the child reacts to a violent video or television movie or violent games. Does the child shy away, react with fictionalizing and distancing, or act out the behavior? The notion that children copy violent scenes exactly is psychologically primitive and based on a simplified image of the soul of the child. The personalities of children have too many layers for a violent image to become directly internalized. There are an array of possible reactions for the soul—assuming a pattern of violence is merely one out of many. As a rule there has to exist a predisposition for violence and violent images.

Examples show that the images for violent behavior can come from the most unexpected areas of life. It is too simple to claim that the media and video games are to blame for the violence of children and teenagers. Children and teenagers indeed act on images, but they probe their entire surroundings and look for it if they already have certain tendencies. They search their environment for images that allow them to express a latent aggressive inclination.

Violent scenes in video games or in the media are fatal only if the child is searching for images in the realm of violence. With the exception of certain extremely brutal videos, which show up on the black market and are difficult even for adults to stomach, videos and the media in themselves do not have a brutalizing effect on children. However violent videos can effect problem children who have low self-esteem and/or are hyper-aggressive. While healthier children either fictionalize, repress or ignore the horrific in movies and television, problem children see a possibility to act out their violence. Violence in the media is not the cause of violent behavior in children but gives certain children a legitimization. They see themselves as Ninja warriors or "homies" because they are looking for a role that will allow them to get out their latent aggressive tendencies. The horror movies and terrible media reports are a source of violent images and fantasies from which the emotionally desperate, socially deprived, and neglected children can draw. The fantasy that by making these horror videos illegal would curb violent incidents is too simplistic. As the Sunday school example shows, there are violent scenarios, roles, and images to be found in any given society. Children and teenagers who are motivated seek them out want to imitate them. The horror movie is not uninhibited, but the imitation of the violence from the video is the expression of the uninhibited. The moral superstructure of healthy children does not break down when they are faced with violence in the media.

Horror scenes and video games pose a new educational challenge to parents and teachers. We now have to help children learn how to responsibly handle these games and media as previously we had to educate children about traffic. If we demonize virtual reality games and horror videos, there is a danger that this area of experience in the child's world will get split off. The moralistic, game-condemning attitude of adults leads to a distancing of the children. They view the agitation and anxiety of adults as hysteria. Since the majority of children and teenagers have the feeling that they can distinguish exactly between reality and fiction, they can only shake their heads at bans and moral decrees. "That's *your* problem," they think and continue through these games to pursue their fascination with violence.

A rigid attitude by the adults results in the children not allowing them to be involved in their interests. The splitting off of this area of experiences can only be prevented when parents and teachers go along with the children. Concretely, this means adults should not instantly throw their hands up in the air, appalled. They should inform themselves about the videos and participate in the games so that they can share their thoughts and feelings with the younger generation. On the one hand, it is a matter of expressing one's own fascination and horror. On the other, it demonstrates an attitude one could have towards this kind of fun. A prudent reaction is suitable. We do not have to view video games as the spawn of the Devil but as a pastime where one's own tendencies towards violence and fascination with violence shimmer through. Children should become aware that adults also feel violence as a possibility within themselves and that they need to come to terms with it over and over again.

A Ballad on the Drive to Mimic

It's true, nothing works so fast as poison!
Man, no matter how underage he might be,
is, as far as the world's vices are concerned,
easily taught and quick to learn.

In February, I don't know which day,
it happened, from just one boy's insistence,
that children, playing in the backyard,
decided to hang Fritzy Nauman.

They knew the stories from the papers,
where murder happens and then the police.
And they decided, to execute Nauman,
because they said he was a thief.

They put his head through a noose.
Complaining a lot, Karl was the pastor,
and told him, if he started to cry,
he would ruin everybody's game.

Fritz Nauman asserted, he was not afraid.
The others were serious and led him on.
The rope was thrown over the carpet pole.
And then one began to hoist Fritzy in the air.

He resisted. It was too late. He was floating.
Then they fastened the rope on the hook.
Fritz twitched, because he was still a bit alive.
A little girl pinched him in the leg.

He wiggled quietly, and a little later
a children's game became murder.
When the seven tiny criminals saw what
they had done, in shock they walked away.

Still nobody knew of the poor child.
The yard was still. The sky was blood-red.
Little Nauman swung in the wind.
He didn't see any of it. Because he was dead.

The widow Zickler, who was shuffling by,
went into the street and started to scream,
although she was not supposed to yell there.
Around six the police appeared.

The mother fainted in front of the boy.
And both were quickly brought in the house.
Karl, who was arrested, coolly said: "We
only did what the grown ups do."

Erich Kästner, 1932

*Author's note: This ballad is based on a newspaper report from
1930.*

CHAPTER THREE

VIOLENCE AND AGGRESSION IN KINDERGARTEN

I magine yourself sitting in a beautiful garden restaurant with your friends. You are having a nice conversation, eating *piccata milanese*[1] and enjoying the evening. Suddenly the person sitting at the table next to you reaches into your spaghetti side dish and throws it to the ground. You object. However your friend does not apologize but grabs your bag and throws it into the street. Fuming with rage you turn on him, whereon your furious dining companion loudly complains about your behavior to the restaurant owner . . . Most likely you imagine something quite different in terms of a pleasant dinner and are not enthusiastic about the behavior of your friend at table.

Such a scenario sounds unlikely. Yet children experience similar situations when they go to kindergarten. What to us may seem like obscure scuffles or unprovoked screaming, in the children's perception there is a narrative behind it. In order to be able to understand how children experience violence and aggression in kindergarten, we have to use our imagination and empathy.

---

[1] Editor's note: this is a delicious Italian dish made with veal and a sharp lemon sauce.

We must put ourselves in their position. Children experience violence and aggression just as dramatically as the hypothetical incident in the restaurant. What seems harmless from an adult perspective is experienced as upsetting by the children. When a six year old girl suddenly is slashed in the palm of her hand by her neighbor during independent work group time, or a boy gets hit in his stomach after showing his buddy that he has a better snack, similar feelings arise in the children as did in the restaurant with us—anger and desperation. If we put ourselves into the world of the child and take their experiences seriously, we notice that violence and aggression present a great challenge both to the kindergarten teacher and to the children. This is a problem with which many kindergarten teachers and children are faced, even if unsuspecting passersby coo in sentimental delight at the sight of a group of little children.

In this chapter we will first look at how violence and aggression is manifested in kindergarten and then examine the position and meaning of the kindergarten teacher. Finally, the kindergarten teacher's various possible reactions to these problems are investigated.

The manifestation of violence and aggression in kindergarten differs from that in school. Since the children are at a different developmental stage, violence and aggression are expressed in a different way. Contrary to what occurs in elementary and high school, kindergarten is more a case of individual children standing out through their violent behavior. Whereas in school, violence and terror often are spread by a group or clique, in kindergarten it usually originates from one or two children. The boy who hits his friend hard over the head with a building block after the two of them had peacefully worked building a garage together and the girl who pushes a friend down the stairs after having been teased by her are typical perpetrators of violent incidents in kindergarten. The aggressive behavior can be identified. Violence expresses itself in unique incidents or actions. Incidents are rare where a subgroup of the kindergarten students become violent or where the entire kindergarten is pulled into violence. One example of the latter is the case where a kindergarten teacher, after briefly having left the room, was met with a hail of slippers upon her return. Another example is the kindergarten girl who was in command of a little gang that specialized in the theft and destruction of toys. Yet contrary to elementary and high school, where violence quickly turns into a group problem, it is individual children who become violent in kindergarten.

What is even more striking in kindergarten rooms is the immediacy of violence. Two children are playing with each other peacefully, the next moment one of the children gets up sobbing and complains that the other child hit him "right in the stomach." Violence in kindergarten has no warning stage, has no extended igniting time in which tension is built up to finally release itself. Suddenly a peaceful setting turns violent.

Many kindergarten children are not aware of their actions. There is no sense of the consequences of their actions and there is a marked lack of conscience. A boy knocks a girl down and then squishes her to the floor with his feet. The upset kindergarten teacher asks him: "Don't you know that hurts?" The boy replies: "No, I'm wearing sneakers!"

Often the violent action is subjectively legitimized because of some little thing. A girl scratches her friend's face because she did not wait up for her. Many children do not realize that their reaction is out of proportion and that a head rap, a punch in the stomach, or a beating with

a stick hurts the other person. "She was giggling stu-
pidly!" is viewed as a legitimate reason for taking violent
action. So, "She shouldn't scream like this!"

Often the children's aggressive behavior contradicts
what they say. In conversation they all oppose violence
but they use it against their classmates anyway. Yet pre-
cisely, that is another matter because "She is wearing stupid patent leather shoes."

In contrast to the school teacher, the kindergarten
teacher gets pulled into the actions and arguments since
they are not kept hidden from him or her. Out of loyalty
to their peers, older children in school often keep silent
and do not tell the teacher. Children in kindergarten will
run all excited up to their teacher yelling "Urs hit me!" or
"Barbara pinched me!" Kindergarten children give away
their classmates and seek the help or cooperation of their
kindergarten teacher. They tell about all the ugly incidents. It is not easy to react correctly as a kindergarten
teacher since even at the slightest incidents some children
show a virtuosity in complaining and demand the
teacher's immediate intervention. The teacher has to decide whether to step in or to leave the conflict resolution
up to the children. It often happens that the complaining
stops when the children become aware that the teacher
cannot be called on for every little incident.

Children tell their incidents to the kindergarten
teacher because in their eyes the teacher shares the responsibility for violence and aggression in the classroom.
The separation between the adult and child's world is not
yet distinct. Kindergarten children expect a reaction from
their teacher. In the fourth grade, violence is often acted
out within one's own subculture, and a child who tells
the teacher is considered a traitor and rejected. When an
incident occurs in kindergarten, however, a teacher's

opinion is needed. Violence is not simply happening in a personal subworld but occurs in the common world. In this common world the children have delegated a particular duty to the kindergarten teacher. The teacher has to draw the line between violence and healthy aggression. The children want the teacher to take a stand. It is not that they will behave accordingly, but the teacher's opinion serves them as a point of orientation in the search for their own attitude. Children need a counter-pole, and this is the kindergarten teacher's position regarding the question of expressing violent impulses and fantasies. The teacher becomes a kindergarten group's moral authority.

Children should learn how to independently draw the line between violence and healthy aggression. To play with Ninja Turtle figures is harmless. To bang around with a stick is barely acceptable, but to pull each other's hair or pull away a chair is not allowed. The children's developmental stage demands that the kindergarten teacher take a stand on violence so that the children learn how to handle violence. When a kindergarten teacher takes over a class, that teacher also takes over the task of defining violence and aggression.

When listening in on kindergarten children's conversations, the teacher's influence becomes apparent. They say things like, "Ms. Lüssi also thinks so. . .", or "Brigitte doesn't want. . ." When kindergarten children talk among themselves, they constantly refer to their kindergarten teacher. With older school children I notice this less often. Of course there the teacher's opinion also plays an important part, but it is considered deplorable to openly refer to the teacher with one's peers.

The difficulty for the kindergarten teacher lies in the need to be in accordance with the children. Children try to look for a position that is usually psychologically understandable. The teacher's attitude has to be in tune with the children's world. What the teacher says has to be acceptable to the children and in accordance with their developmental stage. Utopian or radical visions do not have a chance of being accepted by children.

The dangers of an innocent world view

In fulfilling this task, there are different possibilities. The kindergarten teacher often holds, what I call, an innocent world view. This attitude does not distinguish between real violence and aggression and pretend violence and aggression. As a result, this teacher rejects all play that includes any pretended aggression or violence. There is an outraged reaction when a child raves about being a "He-man," or two boys stage "High Noon" with imaginary pistols in the cloakroom. It is made clear to the children that this kind of play is despised. "What you are doing there is horrible!" Aggression is equaled with real violence.

The problem with this attitude is that children soon develop a feeling of being horrible themselves. When the pleasures of aggressive play and fantasies are pathologized, children feel degenerate as such thoughts go through their minds. When it comes to their own aggressions they have the feeling that they are thinking and acting in a bad way. The kindergarten teacher's innocent world view wants to ban aggression and violence from the child's world. Aggressive fantasies, statements, or stories are regarded the same as violent acts. It is expected of kindergarten children that they only be peaceful and polite with one another. The human Shadow[2] has no place

---

[2] Editor's note: The idea of the Shadow comes from Jungian psychology. It is basically a collection of the hidden, repressed elements of a person and/or culture in an individual or collective psyche.

in kindergarten. For instance, there was even a kindergarten teacher who wanted to prevent her children from hearing about the fact that the class cat was run over by a car. The horrible is blocked out.

However, such an innocent world view carries great psychological dangers. Unfortunately it is not the case that children copy this behavior on a one to one scale. Aggression gets split off. The children notice that, for their kindergarten teacher, violence and aggression are themes filled with complexes. They keep silent. They register their kindergarten teacher's view, notice how she or he reacts with dismay at a brawl and finds "Skeletor" disgusting. They start to hide their aggressive fantasies. On the surface, better behaved children adapt to their teacher while actually hiding their Shadow in fear of releasing it. They feel that their kindergarten teacher's orientation is based on an innocent world fantasy and feel isolated in their fascination with violence. The dialogue with the child's Shadow is blocked. The pleasures of a tank cannot be expressed, and the play shooting with a toy pistol has to be repressed.

The innocent world reaction can hide behind a mental externalization of violence. When violent incidents occur in kindergarten, an external reason is sought out, family conflicts for example, and declared as the cause. The aggressive boy is surely being abused by a parent. The stubborn girl is not looked after and is watching violent videos at home. The search for causes and the societal background of violent behavior in children is of eminent importance, but the acting-out of the Shadow may be independent of these causes. Therefore the Shadow connected with it must not be ignored. We should make an effort to recognize familiar connections, while at the same time be aware that we run the danger of explaining away violence in kindergarten children as well as within ourselves. The chance of us recognizing our part in the violence is reduced through this externalization.

Interestingly, many parents have a similar reaction regarding violence. They also externalize the cause of violence. Their child, of course, is never responsible for violence. It is another's influence, the atmosphere in the kindergarten, the other children, a "difficult boy" in the class, or the way in which the kindergarten is run.

However, we must start with the assumption that aggression belongs to human nature. Pleasure in destruction and violence is an ancient, human *ur*-quality. Not always can outer circumstances—the family, the environment—be held responsible for a child's aggressive tendencies. Of course there is a hidden cry for help behind a child's violent behavior, but many times it is mixed with a genuine delight in violence and destruction. When violent incidents occur in kindergarten, both aspects should be considered. Violence can be an indicator of disharmony, a family problem or inadequate living conditions. At the same time however, it has an *ur*-fascination. The innocent world reaction leads to a fatal repression of this *ur* or original pleasure in aggressive fantasies and games. It makes it difficult for children to draw the necessary line between violence and aggression. The Shadow, or the horrible in humanity, has no thematic space.

Therefore, paradoxically, a pronounced innocent world view can promote aggression in children. In a kindergarten class, a slightly overweight child was catagorically being avoided and then was bombarded with pine cones during a field trip. The kindergarten teacher decided to have a talk with all the children. For almost an entire hour she appealed to their conscience and told them, from now on, to be nice to the girl. Afterwards in the jacket room she heard the children agree to "Destroy her!" These children felt an inner obligation to live out their other side. They wanted to bring the Shadow or dark side into kindergarten or their world. If the kindergarten teacher does not provide for that possibility, the children will refuse to obey or, at best, introduce the Shadow in a different form. For example, there was the case of a boy who, when asked a question that should have been answered "one," held up his middle finger towards his teacher with a grin.[3]

The kindergarten teacher's monopoly on violence

How should one behave as a kindergarten teacher when violent incidents occur? As contrasted to middle and high school level teachers, the kindergarten teacher has the advantage that the monopoly on violence lies firmly in his or her hands. The kindergarten teacher's power position is unquestioned. From the children's point of view, the kindergarten teacher possesses the necessary means to dominate. The teacher commands respect through an obvious immense physical dominance. The mere knowledge of the kindergarten teacher's superiority is enough to stop outbursts of violence amongst children. The twice as large and four times as strong being has the ability to pick them up, shake them vigorously, pull them by their hair or send them out of the room. This is a form of reacting that is not available to a high school teacher. Thanks to physical superiority, the kindergarten teacher takes on a special position. Even when physical intimidation is not being used, the children still perceive their teacher in this way. The teacher can separate two fighting children or put an aggressive child outside the

---

[3] Editor's note: In other words the boy gave her the finger.

door. The kindergarten teacher can react more forcefully than other teachers, thanks to a monopoly on violence.

This monopoly on violence is of course never allowed to become the core of pedagogic work. We cannot force children's participation exclusively on the basis of our superiority but, psychologically, it is of great significance to them. The children believe that the kindergarten teacher possesses violence—even if the kindergarten teacher does not subjectively perceive it in this way.

If the line is crossed, if unacceptable incidents occur, then, from the children's perspective, there is a threat that the kindergarten teacher will make use of the monopoly on violence and step in. This is also sensed by the kindergarten teacher. A slip of the hand can quickly happen where a child gets pulled by the hair or another one receives a spanking. Because of the monopoly on violence held by the kindergarten teacher, such moral lapses are more likely to occur in kindergarten than in school grades, where such moral lapses would be prevented by an anticipated strong reaction of the students.

From the children's perspective, the kindergarten teacher is the focus of kindergarten. The teacher is perceived as the psychological center, compared to certain school classes, where the teacher is only a marginal figure and the peer leaders are the ones that count. The kindergarten teachers personality has a direct effect on the atmosphere in the kindergarten. The children adjust to the kindergarten teacher's mood. They perceive a teacher's feelings, what is going on inside and react accordingly. The kindergarten teacher is a center point through which the children can discover other children and themselves. Often the children become attuned to one another in the room through their teacher, and the group of children can reflect the kindergarten teacher's emotional state.

This role does not make every day life easy for the kindergarten teacher. Personal energies have to be drawn upon in order to create a good kindergarten.

What does this mean in terms of violence? The way a kindergarten teacher approaches violence effects the class. Internal turbulence, personal problems, or conflicts create an unsettled atmosphere. The children can sense what is going on inside their kindergarten teacher and react to it. They become wild and stubborn. They quarrel and fight. They feel it if something is not right with their kindergarten teacher. If violence occurs in the kindergarten room, the teacher always has to ask the question, "What does this have to do with me? Am I nervous, inconsistent, in bad emotional shape?" There has to be a turning inwards to recognize one's part in the children's violence.

The kindergarten teacher's internal turbulence becomes fatal when he or she believes that it is possible to get around uneasy feelings. "I'm fine! I'm not aggressive, I don't have any problems!" Such an attitude irritates the children. They consequently try to provoke the kindergarten teacher. They behave miserably so that the dishonest façade collapses. When the teacher finally starts yelling, it is received with relief. "Finally she is getting mad. We knew she was in a bad mood!" The kindergarten teacher's bad moods and hidden aggressions are a kindergarten child's opportunity. Through these moods the children can bring in their own Shadows. If the kindergarten teacher is not in good emotional shape and can admit that to the children, the children and the teacher can then together articulate the more difficult aspects of human existence. This way violence and aggression become a mutual subject, not split off from adults and solely left to the children.

The you-should-think *attitude: taking limited responsibility*

Ethnic conflicts and the fear of foreigners are other problems which confront kindergarten and school children. This can lead to outbursts of violence.

A Turkish girl joined a kindergarten class. She hardly spoke German. The kindergarten teacher was not greatly concerned about her integration, assuming that another well assimilated Turkish girl and boy would certainly help her out. The kindergarten teacher decided to do her best in helping to promote the contact between these children. What happened? The new, younger Turkish girl was ignored by the other children, chased after class and even beaten up once or twice. A negative dynamic developed towards the new foreigner. The girl was completely intimidated and finally even refused to talk. In conversation the children were insightful and promised to take more care of the girl but the resolutions were soon forgotten. A hatred of foreigners? The kindergarten teacher took a closer look at the other two Turkish children's behavior and discovered that not only did these two Turkish children behave with a complete lack of solidarity towards their compatriot, but systematically egged on the other children to attack her. They encouraged the others to tease her and helped to beat her up. The reason was finally found; the new girl was Kurdish (and not Turkish).

Ethnic conflicts manifest themselves in kindergartens over and over again. Children initiate fights over rivalries and animosities that they experienced in their country. Croats are against Serbs, Kurds against Turks, and even Cambodians against Vietnamese. They bring the conflict that they know from their country and their parents into kindergarten. Indirectly the kindergarten teacher witnesses this conflict and of course wants to do the very best to improve the situation.

But what can be done? Many ideas and feelings come up. It seems logical to tackle the problem at its roots, and the efforts should focus on the causes. This *one-should* thinking, although well intentioned, is also dangerous. It does not only show up in ethnic conflicts but also with other identified causes of aggression and violence: *one-should* prohibit violent videos, *one-should* educate parents in parenting before they become fathers or mothers, *one-should* prohibit "game-boy" and so on. We put demands on our society, on politicians, and finally on the world itself. It is indeed important to see the larger connection, yet the danger with this kind of thinking is that we avoid our own responsibility. We recognize, see, and know all connections, think universally and connectedly, and at the same time forget to act in the smaller realm where we have an effect. We cannot singlehandedly solve the problems of our society and the world. We must prevent that feeling of universal responsibility that causes us to overlook the possibilities in our own milieu.

For kindergarten teachers this means that they should be limited to their own field of activity. This is true even when feeling that the inadequate parents are actually at fault, video consumption is brutalizing the child, or an ethnic conflict is at play. Associative thinking is important because it widens the horizon and increases the ability to recognize connections but, on a pedagogic level, linking violence to societal influences can lead to stasis. We pull back since we cannot solve the problems in any way. The *one-should-thinking* creates a feeling of impotence. We resign and withdraw into privacy.

As individuals we cannot be responsible for the entire world. It is important however that we recognize our limited responsibility and act where we have the possibility of success with ourselves as well as in the small area of a kindergarten. Here it is a question of acting, even if the fundamental conflicts are not solved and the underlying causes escape our control. The kindergarten teacher has the duty to react, to give oneself to the work, to participate, to talk, and to reflect on personal aggression with the awareness of only being able to accomplish a little in the larger scope of things. Yet this attention can make a meaningful contribution. The aforementioned kindergarten teacher could not of course make the feelings of animosity carried around by children from different ethnic groups disappear. But she did achieve an overall atmosphere in which this conflict did not have to be disputed over and over again and where the other children were not dragged under by it.

CHAPTER FOUR

THE FEARS OF CHILDREN AND TEENAGERS

Fear belongs to one of the existential categories of experiences that we, as humans, cannot avoid. However our attitude towards fear is divided. Consciously we try to live a fear free life, avoiding danger and horror so that fear does not even surface. At the same time, we feel an incredible fascination for it. We are thrilled when reading a horrifying *whodunit* or watching a scary movie. We want to experience fear without really being threatened. This desire for fear makes children race down dangerous streets on their skateboards, climb trees, or threaten each other. Boys particularly seek out the horrible which seems to invigorate them and awaken their senses.

While fear remains an anthropological constant, its outward manifestations or triggering factors change. For example, when the first trains appeared many people panicked at the sight of these monsters. Consequently doctors came to say that riding trains was bad for your health. In the 50's fear of flying was widespread. On even the shortest domestic flight, one or two passengers would throw up. Today the fear of flying has decreased considerably. At the moment we fear exposure to sun rays, over radiated or poisoned food, and air pollution. The outward manifestations of fear are influenced by the *zeitgeist* and current events. The face of fear and its causes are forever changing. With fear it is always a challenge. We have to confront fear like Sisyphus (who had to push a rock up a mountain over and over again) knowing that we will never be able to conquer it.

This chapter will describe contemporary manifestations of fear in children and teenagers. An attempt will be made to elaborate on their typical fears. Following this, the coping strategies mobilized by children and teenagers will be outlined.

The personal horror scenario

Beat[1] is an alert, intelligent, ten year old student. He is about to make the change from elementary school to the next grade level in middle school. The teacher is convinced that he will be able to master middle school without any problems. He will surely not have any problems adapting. No one has any doubts that Beat will be a good middle school student. Suddenly however Beat's behavior changes. His grades at school start to decrease severely. He does his homework unwillingly and for the most part sloppily. He hardly participates in class any more. His teacher and parents are astounded. Beat declares that he does not want to go to middle school; it is not for him. This sudden behavior and change of mind has everyone concerned. What is the matter with him?

As a psychological counselor, I try to examine, through conversations, drawings and observations, what the emotional causes of these sudden changes in attitude and behavior could be. What has happened to this boy? There are no recognizable changes in his environment. His parents are supportive and lovingly care for him.

---

[1] Translator's note: This is a common Swiss name for boys. It is pronounced *bey-aat.*

What is going on inside the boy remains a mystery until our third session. While we are saying good-bye, he casually mentions that he has parked his bicycle on Mulberry street right next to the indoor pool. I ask him whether he likes to swim. The boy hesitates and becomes quiet. I become suspicious. Finally we start a conversation about swimming and swimming lessons. Without looking me in the eye, he confesses that he hates the diving board. He particularly fears the three meter diving board. He knows that diving from the 3 meter board is a requirement in middle school, and he has seen the swimming instructor force a middle school student do so. The scene has made an impression on him. It becomes obvious that Beat does not want to enter middle school because he is afraid of the jump. His decline in grades and sudden change of attitude were caused by the idea of having to jump into the deep from this height.

Beat's behavior is typical of many older children and teenagers. Of course not all of them are afraid to jump, but it is typical that they keep their private fears to themselves. To express fear is just as embarrassing to them as it is to express other intimate feelings such as a first love, body anxieties or social insecurities. How could Beat admit that at the mere thought of having to dive from 3 meters he starts shaking? Everyone would laugh at him, so he kept quiet. I also observed this kind of behavior in open, extroverted children who are eager to communicate and warmly open to their teacher and parents. Such children often express feelings of fear. For example, Beat was greatly concerned about acid rain killing the forests and the war in Bosnia-Herzegovina. Outwardly it appeared that he was expressing all of his fears, but in reality, he kept part of them to himself.

Older children adapt their verbal fears to the environment and parental fantasies. Beat's example is typical of children. Often these remarks do not correspond with the fears that float around in their heads. What they say reflects the way in which the environment handles fears and not the feelings that really concern them. It is also difficult for these children to express their innate fears. Rationally they often realize that they should not be afraid. They recognize that their fear has no rational base—the construction worker digging in the school yard is not going to throw them into a pit or the doctor is not going to discover their "snot" when they stand in front of the x-ray machine—however, their uneasy feelings do not leave them. Beat also realizes that it is ridiculous to be afraid of jumping off the diving board, but his fear remains. Children and teenagers are blocked in their development through these kind of secret fears and become incapable of taking on challenges suitable to their age. They block themselves internally.

What subjectively may be experienced as the reason for fear by a child could still have a deeper meaning. Of course it is not actually the jump that is causing Beat's fear, but unconsciously he has chosen an image that expresses an existential feeling of fear. We have to reverse our perspective and view Beat's fear not causally but teleologically. The fears of this phase of his life are concentrated in the diving board. The fear of jumping is not simply the cause of his fears and not the actual reason for the decline in his school grades. But at his age his soul has picked the diving board as the place loaded with meaning. He needs an image to give shape to an existential feeling. Maybe Beat chose this object to express his fear of the future. An experience with a new class was awaiting him. As a soon-to-be eleven year old boy, developing from a child into a teenager, he fears what is coming towards him. He is afraid of not being able to handle the expectations and challenges of the future. This feeling is present in him but diffuse. The feeling chooses an object in order to express itself. Therefore the fear of the diving board is to be taken both literally and symbolically. The jump into life, into the next life—meaning middle school—causes fear.

What could be the deeper background behind this dynamic? In order to answer this question and to illuminate ways to deal with it, it is helpful to focus on non-European cultures. As described by Van Gennep,[2] Mircea Eliade[3] and Joseph Campbell,[4] many cultures have specific transitional rituals when moving from childhood into young adulthood and from young adulthood into adulthood. The child has to be able to pass tests in order to enter into the next phase of life. For example, the four year old children of the Omaha tribe in Nebraska have to undergo a special ceremony recognizing that they are not little children any more and are now allowed to wear sandals. In this ceremony-*the turning of the child*-their hair is cut, and among the teepees they are challenged to walk on a straight line from one point to another. While they are taking their steps, special songs, reserved only for this ceremony, are sung. As described by Alice Fletcher and Francis La Flesche,[5] children fear this ritual. They are afraid and not sure whether they will pass the

---

[2] Van Gennep, *Übergangsriten* (Frankurt: Campus, 1981).

[3] Mircea Eliade, *Rites and Symbols of Initiation*, tr. Willard Trask (1958; rpt. Woodstock, Connecticut: Spring Publications, 1995).

[4] Joseph Campell, *The Way of the Animal Powers* (London: Harper & Row, 1983).

[5] Alice Fletcher & Francis La Flesche, *The Omaha Tribe*, Vol. 1& 2 (Lincoln: University of Nebraska Press, 1972).

test. If they fail to stay on the line, it is seen as a bad omen.

In other such ceremonies of initiation rituals, boys are tortured before they are considered adults. Among the aborigines in northern Australia, the initiates have to lie in the sun for hours until they are almost completely dehydrated before they are told the secrets of the tribe. What stands out in all of these initiation ceremonies is that they are connected to fear. The children are scared and challenged to overcome their fear.

Within Beat's hidden fear of jumping from the diving board, there is concealed an existential fear of life's next phase. Given the lack of other cultural ceremonies which could capture this feeling, Beat has unconsciously chosen a situation and place that will allow him to enact a private initiation. The diving board for him becomes the touchstone, the point of resistance, which he chooses to use for his further development. His fear of the diving board therefore signifies that he is ready for the next phase in his growth. Unconsciously, he chooses an angst filled situation in order to step into the next part of his life. His decline in grades is therefore not simply to be seen pathologically but in relation to his internal preparation for the future.

What is problematic here is that all of this takes place in secret. Beat's fear is not contained and respected by a community but has to be kept to himself. It should be the duty of education to develop ceremonies based on these fears that children have.

We particularly face a problem here with younger children. For the most part, there is little room left for scenarios through which they can express their personal fears. We socialize children according to our fears—traffic, hygiene, sex—concrete fears. If we ask them to be afraid where sound dangers prevail, they adapt to our fears. However, we lack ceremonies where children are confronted with their own fears, and where they can put them into images appropriate for their age. We have few ceremonies where fear can be experienced collectively. Fear as a mutual experience has been desocialized excepting perhaps watching movies and television. With the idea of a "fear free childhood" we avoid sharing fearful experiences. We do not have proper ceremonies through which fears can be experienced and overcome according to age. We demand that children adapt to our realities. As a consequence, children secretly look for hidden situations to express their feelings. They do not communicate their fears and this brings with it the danger of stagnation. A conflict is repressed, and a challenge is not taken.

Controlled fright: children's attempts to overcome fear

How should one react to children's fears? How can we prevent this split between expressed feelings and actual fears? A possible answer is with rituals.

> In the evening, when I went to bed I often was terribly afraid. I believed that someone could climb into my room from outside and abduct me. I then however invented a strategy. Before I went to bed I lined up toy soldiers in front of my window. They stood there with their guns and tanks. I placed a lamp so that it would throw a little light on them. When I then went to bed, I imagined they were protecting me. This way I could fall asleep peacefully.

A different example is:

> I could only fall asleep after my father told me a story. Often they were frightening stories. My favorite was

the story about the giant Turramulli.[6] After this horror story I would lie in bed for awhile, go to the bath-
room one more time or to the kitchen to get a glass of
water, before I could finally go to sleep.

Such going to sleep rituals are well known. They are
ways in which children try to master their own fears.
They develop a series of acts, rituals, that are always
played out in the same way and that banish fear. These
rituals become familiar while at the same time provoking
a slight thrill. Children invent their own rituals without
the help of parents or educators. Yet rituals can be constellated through the involvement with a mother or father. The mother who gives her son an apple to take to
kindergarten everyday is participating in a ritual. She
makes it easier for the child to separate from home.
Such rituals are important for different reasons. They
bring the children's fears into existence. The terrible is
not banished but finds its place in a series of actions. On
the one hand the boy who lines up toy soldiers experiences the dimension of the terrifying, while on the other
he tests a procedure that can be mobilized when afraid.
Fear is present but turns into an occasion for a counter-
measure. With the second example there is the opportunity of the father's participation in the ritual. The child
experiences thrilling feelings when hearing the story but
knows that he is not alone. The feelings of fear are permitted within the relationship and in addition have their
place in the "horror" story (which could also be a
fairytale). Paradoxically this has a calming effect. The
shared ritual prevents the fears from becoming
impenetrable or diffused. The important fact is that the
father shares the fears with his child. When telling the

---

[6] Trezise & Roughen, Göttingen 1990.

story he allows for a little bit of fear in order to be able to overcome it together with his son. The child can place his fears and learn from the father how to distance himself from them. The mutually experienced thrill helps to overcome fears. If the father were to mislead the child into believing that there was no need for fear, he would be deceitful. It is an illusion to believe that children can grow up without fear. They meet up with fear both as an internal and external threat. We can not keep the horrors of the world from our children.

Instead of hiding personal fears and misleading children into believing that a fear free life is possible, it is better for adults to experience fear together with a child. Early on in education there needs to be a confrontation with fear so that the child can learn ways of coping. Often mothers and fathers orient themselves on a sentimental image of the child. Instead of taking on fear and trying to share it with the child, the focus is fixated on the cause. The child cannot fall asleep *because* the neighbors cat got run over. The daughter is afraid of school *because* the bad boys are threatening her. Fear as an internal reality is not excepted. Of course these external reasons are part of creating fear, but fear should not be dealt with through these external causes alone. When a child is afraid, it is not only a question of rejecting the fear, fear should be seen as an opportunity to develop common ceremonies that will strengthen the child's ego and aid in entering into a dialogue with the child's own fears.

The drowned canary—neurotic forms of fear

Up until now, descriptions were related to average, normal fears in children. In the following pages, neurotic developments of fear and loathing will be described. These are particularily the behaviors behind which unresolved fears are suspected.

Peter is a ten year old boy who moved from the Lakeland region in Switzerland to Bern with his family. In school he is a loner. The teacher describes him as inaccessible. The other children either avoid him or catch him and beat him up. He has difficulties making friends. His mother thinks that he behaves rather passively at home. He does not know what to do with himself on his free afternoons and sits in his room bored. His only real interest is his canary. It was a present given to him by his older sister and he lovingly cares for it. One morning the mother finds the bird dead in the sink of the boy's room. The incident upsets the parents. What happened? Obviously the bird had been drowned. There is a feeling of helplessness. Could it have been Peter? The incident also alarms the older sister. Something is wrong with this boy. The thing that Peter must have done is unthinkable. How is it possible that Peter drowned his loved bird?

During therapy sessions with Peter, words are scarce. Mostly he only sits looking around the room apathetically and does his homework reluctantly. In school his condition worsens. He does not seem to care about anything. Yet occasionally he has aggressive fits. He destroys his pencils or suddenly rips his notebooks apart. Because I am not getting anywhere with the boy, I seek out an intensive collaboration with the mother, father, and sister. They are confronted with the suspicion that the boy could be heavily burdened internally. Something is disturbing him. Is it an experience from the past, a problem at school, or an unexpressed family conflict? After a couple of conversations, I learn that his change in personality started a year ago after moving to Bern. He used to be much livelier, but he is acting differently now that they live in Bern. The family has an explanation at hand regarding Peter's change in behavior, namely the move. Unanimously they all solemnly declare that country life obviously is nicer. Peter is simply a country boy. This unanimity makes me skeptical. Country life is praised as paradise while city life almost belongs to the devil. A comment from the sister finally helps me along. She casually mentions an incident that took place at the bus depot, an insignificant incident according to her. A bus driver had invited the boy to ride with him to the bus depot. That evening Peter had come home disturbed and was quiet and sullen during the following days. Something must have happened at the bus depot. Later this bus driver was arrested for sexually molesting children. The family now suspects that something terrible might have happened to Peter.

The news in the paper about the arrest hit the family like a bomb. Yes, Peter must have had a terrible experience with the driver. Both mother and father suspected sexual abuse but did not dare express their fears or ask the boy for details. The awful suspicion became a taboo because such an incident could not be tolerated in this family. It would have destabilized the home life. Of course, the boy sensed that he was being accused of something terrible. The shadow of sexual abuse hovered over the entire family. Since the family neither possessed a sexual language nor a reasonably open attitude towards sex, not a word was allowed to be spoken regarding this incident. It was too awful. When addressed on this subject, the mother would react nervously saying that all these stories about sexual abuse were just media hype.

It was impossible to find out what really happened at the bus depot. This did not matter psychologically. The assumed or real incident at the bus depot triggered a family complex: sexuality. This was being repressed out of a pious attitude. Everything sexual was considered indecent. Even if Peter was innocent, through the occurrence at the bus depot he was being identified with this complex. Peter became the carrier of the family's sexual shame. The family had projected a personal conflict onto him. Unconsciously, according to their rigid attitude, they regarded him as guilty and dirty. The possible abuse put the boy into the position of being the taboo breaker. Peter sensed this dynamic and suffered greatly. This non-verbalized suspicion awakened fears in him. He felt guilty because at the same time he was battling with his own sexual fantasies. He was probably having suicidal thoughts. In desperation he finally chose an action in order to relieve the internal psychological pressure. The drowning of his canary was an attempt confront the family's unspoken accusations. To get rid of his guilt, he killed the bird instead of himself. He made a sacrifice to his family. Whether or not sexual abuse occurred at the bus depot became irrelevant. The fact of the matter is that the parents' fears were enough to trigger a negative family dynamic and burden Peter in the deepest possible way.

What does this conflict show us of children's fears? Peter was emotionally over challenged. He had to surmount a family problem. He became identified with demonic sexuality because of the incident at the bus depot. The fears from which he suffered were released by the family's diffused demand to solve their horror of sexuality. Peter became a threat to the family.

Peter's behavior is typically observed in children. An unexpressed something is in the air—a fear in the family or a fear in school. The child senses this and becomes uneasy. The child suffers because the subject is not talked about. Again, for example, a girl began burying her dolls. Her surprised mother noticed that the eight year old had taken on her mother's fear of her husband having a heart attack. Often an external expression is needed so that fear can show itself. With the boy, it was the incident at the bus depot. With the girl, it was the funeral of a great uncle that she had taken part in that triggered the macabre game of burying her dolls. Often it is the children that activate these fears through an experience.

Overcoming fear through self-sacrifice

A different, negative way of overcoming fear can lead to a destructive development of the Self. This happens when an unresolved fear, *a priori*, makes it impossible for the child to find a positive identity.

Paola was three years old when she came to Switzerland. She was adopted by Swiss parents who lovingly cared for her. In elementary school she showed artistic talent. She could draw beautifully. In fourth grade an inner anxiety started to take hold of her. She became rebellious towards her teacher, smart mouthed and unapproachable. Though at times she could be friendly and more-or-less well adjusted. By sixth grade her rebellious behavior escalated and turned into open aggression. If something did not suit her, she would burst into wild insults. She began to be absent from school. She started hanging out and staying away from home. The girl said she was possessed by the devil. She rejected any help, and her only wish in life was to become a prostitute. She wanted nothing to do with miserable social workers with their mournful eyes.

After talks with Paola, her parents, and teachers, it became clear that she had constructed a personal myth for herself. She claimed that she actually was a South American vagabond. She viewed herself as lost and doomed. She was dominated by the fixed idea that she would not be able to develop a positive identity here, that there was no room for her in society. Ultimately though, her behavior was determined by fear. She was afraid of failure, afraid of failing in life. In addition, a low self-esteem resulted in her not realizing her potential, and she fled into fantasies of the future. She gave up on herself in order to prevent personal failure. As paradoxical as this may sound, she overcame fear by giving in to her darkest fantasies. Secretly she feared life's challenges, and she tried to conquer those fears by bringing on the catastrophe.

Paola connected her contemporary situation with her past. She believed her first three years in life and her origins to be the source of her problems. Whether or not she had experienced an early trauma is not important. She developed a negative identity. Out of fear of life she orientated herself with a negative self-image. By viewing herself as lost, she gave herself up to the destructive fantasies that she actually feared. She produced a destructive story for herself. Unfortunately such self-destructive individuation is common among teenagers. They give in to the fascination of the terrifying not only out of fear of failure but also out of protest or because of unresolved conflicts. Their development does not go in a positive direction but spirals down into the deepest abyss of the underworld. They give into all the temptations that parents and teachers warn them against. With frightening persistence they insist on experiencing the terrible in life even when there is the danger of self-disintegration. Salvation is looked for in the drug scene or in the excesses of violence. Meanwhile a healthy, normal way of life is regarded as deadly or boring. In Los Angeles members of the "Crips" and "Bloods," the two most prominent gangs of the city, emphasize that only a real murder gives meaning to life.[7] In this perverse subculture murder becomes a

---

[7] Léon Bing: *Do or Die*, see above.

step in individuation, a possibility of becoming oneself in the attempt to overcoming internal despair. As a child and juvenile psychologist, it is often difficult to influence such teenagers because they are driven by an almost fanatical conviction that they are going in the only possible direction . They destroy themselves out of fear of life.

It is important for us to listen carefully when such behavior occurs. Destructive behavior, hyper-agressiveness, or resignation can all be warning signs. The unconscious is working on a negative script through which fear is being dealt. As a child psychologist, educator, mother, or father a great deal of sensitivity and fantasy are needed in order to be able to touch the emotional undertexture. What superficially looks like a behavioral problem can turn out to be an unconscious way of overcoming fear.

Wild Franz

Franz as a boy would get little birds,
Strangle them, and their pain
For him was pleasure. Everyone scrammed
When someone shouted, "Wild Franz is coming!"

No beast was safe from him. He
Went, like a murderer, always around.
Never was his look cheerful,
Unless he had done some evil.

As a boy he chilled his rage
Only in the warm blood of poor beasts.
But what's done when young is done when old,
Still bloodthirsty he was as a man.

Once beasts, he now murders
People.—Children, look there.
There on the gallows his skull
Shines now in the pale moonlight.

Johann Michael Armbruster

CHAPTER FIVE

PARENTS FEARING THEIR CHILDREN

The title of this chapter seems monstrous. Fear of one's own children? We are plagued with different personal fears: fear of traffic accidents, diseases, of failing an exam, or of death. We are afraid of dangers like environmental catastrophes or loosing our jobs. Furthermore, we suffer from non-specific anxieties. We cannot fall asleep at night. Or we have the feeling that we cannot live up to expectations or that we have done everything wrong. Fear is a feeling or an emotional state with which we are greatly familiar . Traditionally women have tended to try to avoid fear, while men seem to have tried to control it. Today mountain climbing or "bungy-jumping" makes it possible to experience fear and overcome it at the same time.

We are familiar with fears—but do we have to fear our own children? Are not children those people who are closest to us? The ones that we love and wish to have a happy life? If we fear our own children, there is something wrong with the world. In normal relationships, under normal circumstances—whatever that may mean exactly—we should not be afraid of our own children. The relationship must be dysfunctional. Take for example the couple who had to ask for police protection on their silver wedding anniversary. Their son threatened to shoot the guests if they had a party. Or how about the father who was robbed by his drug addicted daughter and her friends. In such extreme situations fear is justifiable, but when circumstances are more or less intact, fear seems uncalled for.

The starting point in this chapter will not begin with such extreme cases but instead will examine normal relationships. We will take up the question of what it means to fear our own children, and whether these feelings are at all justifiable. Are children today behaving in such a way that we have to fear them? We will see that fearing one's children is an important quality in the relationship between parents, children, and teachers.

Where does the fear of our children come from? We fear our children because we hear of incidents that occur in children and youth groups. In one school a strange game developed called "containerle.[1]" This game was invented by a girl in fifth grade. A smaller child was stuck into a box, and then it would be pushed around wildly in the neighborhood and the captured child would scream. For more fun two children would throw burning newspapers into the container while the child was still in it.

When we hear of such incidents we get chills down our spines. Most of the time parents and or teachers are not aware of such activities. The children keep it to themselves. They are loyal to their peers. What happens at game time is not meant for the ears of the adults. Do we have to be afraid of our children?

The problem of the parent-child relationship

Before we get into this question, we should reflect on the parent-child relationship. Parent-child relationships

---

[1] Translator's note: This is a German verb meaning to put into a container or box.

are not like holiday acquaintances where we communicate with each other through our sunny sides and where the euphoric atmosphere lends a pink hue to the other. Maintaining a parent-child relationship is the hardest of work. In it we are constantly confronted with our feelings, emotional states, and complexes. The parent-child relationship is difficult and problematic even in its origins. The tensions, conflicts, fears, and ambivalence that happen between children and parents are already described for us in the Bible. Abraham is willing to sacrifice his son to God. Jacob betrays his blind father Isaac by pretending to be Esau. Absalom, the third son of King David, organizes a revolt against his father. Fathers in the Bible have to fear their children and vice versa.

In Shakespeare's *King Lear*, it is Lear's two daughters who treat their father atrociously. Lear gives his kingdom to his daughters, Goneril and Regan, under their promise that he may live back and forth between them. Breaking their promise, Lear is rejected by them. Only the youngest daughter, Cordelia, to whom Lear did not give anything, takes pity on her mad father.

The parent-child relationship is under a double strain. Parents form a psychological unity with their children. While this allows for security and trust, it also involves great difficulties and psychological challenges. Parent-child relationships are difficult because parents are emotionally connected to their children. The family forms a community that is consciously and unconsciously connected on many levels. Family members enact dramas on one another without actually being aware of it.

The notion that the family should be an intense living entity has increased in the last decades. Father, mother, and children no longer have their traditional roles through which they move in their own realms of life.

Instead, boundaries are now mixed. With my own grandparents, it used to be customary that children would have to disappear into the cellar and play. The noise and excitement of the grandchildren was tiresome to the adults and disturbed their conversation. We children rarely ate at the same table as the adults. Contrary to education thirty or more years ago, we now try to form a living and educational unity with our children. The father's duty is no longer limited to a quick good night kiss. Many modern fathers are integrated into the family in that he chases after his small son who refuses to go to bed, or looks for the "pingu[2]" without which his daughter will not fall asleep. He also spends time in the kitchen or devotes his leisure time to his children. Of course not all families have a strict division of responsibilities, but according to contemporary belief, the husband is to participate in housekeeping and the upbringing of the children. The role of mothers has expanded as well. Interests and duties outside the home are more common. The modern mother does not always have to be cooped up at home busy in the kitchen. Eating habits within the family have also changed. Children eat together with adults.

Not only do we live in a tight community with our children, but as father or mother, we also want to dedicate ourselves to their education! This is no longer being exclusively delegated to nannies, schools or other outside authorities. More and more education is being carried out by the parents themselves. These are reasons why people first think of the parents when a child misbehaves. "The father should . . . , Why didn't the mother . . . ?" In several schools, parents' night is considered important. In

---

[2] Translator's note: This is a child's nickname for a stuffed penguin. It would be equivalent to an American's "teddy" for a stuffed bear.

a family with three or four children this soon develops scheduling problems. Here the attitude has changed. Until the sixties it was uncommon that parents would talk the education of their child over with the teachers. Children were sent alone to their first day of school.

The separation between the adult's world and the child's world has been dissolved. The family is no longer a place where everybody lives in their own well defined section—mother in the kitchen, the children in their rooms, and father in his study—but the territories are mixed. This shows itself also in the realm of leisure time. Children are left to themselves even less in their leisure time. Free time serves as an opportunity to do something together with the children; a mutual bicycle excursion, a trip to the public swimming pool, or a vacation together.

I have no objections to these changes, and many readers will have probably welcomed these new family forms. We do not want back the kind of family where the parents did not concern themselves with the children except to rear them, where the father stood out through his internal and external absence, and where, in well to do families, children were handed over to nannies. It is easy for us to say good-by to all of that. As positive as this development may be, it still has brought with it some dangers and additional challenges that we have not kept in mind. If we want to live together with our children, as well bring them up, we have to be able to deal with the new, psychologically complicated situation. We can no longer keep the children at a distance and close ourselves off from their different sides and qualities, yet we are confronted with all the aspects of their personalities.

A father takes his two sons to the *Sechseläuten*[3] children's parade, a spring festival in Zürich. They admire
the beautifully decorated floats and costumes that pass by
them. Contentedly he strolls with his sons to the tram
stop. Suddenly the eight and ten year old boys pull away
and run to the other end of the station. The boys are be-
side themselves and shout, "cool!" They have discovered a
variety of machine guns, toy grenades and military
planes. They eagerly pull at the plastic bags with the war
toys. They hop up and down and demand that their father buy at least one set for them. *Sechseläuten* and the
wonderful parade are forgotten. Horrified, the father
wants to turn away. He is obviously disgusted and wants
nothing to do with what is interesting his children. He
tries to pull them away whereon screaming and shouting
breaks out. The father receives hateful stares from the
people around. The harmonious atmosphere has evapo-
rated, an abyss has opened up. The sons have become
strangers to the father. He is angry.

The father has let himself enter into a relationship
with his children. Yet he is experiencing the development
of interests in his children that he opposes. He is confronted with all aspects of his children's personalities. His
relationship with his children results in him getting to
know both their bright and hidden sides. It is difficult for
him to remain neutral because he is emotionally connected to his children.

Entering into a relationship is always dangerous. Deep
human relationships are often marked by ambivalence. If
we really want to engage the *other*, and additionally be

---

[3] Editor's note: This festival celebrates the end of winter and the start
of spring. It is highlighted by parades and culminates in an archaic
ritual burning of a snowman on a pyre in the central square of
Bellevue.

connected emotionally with this *other*—as in the family—the facade often crumbles. A variety of feelings emerge. On one hand, great qualities show themselves, and on the other, the pits of the human soul open up. Love and hate break through. There is violence, aggression, rage, and desperation, but there is also joy and community. The violent and murderous in us shows itself as do our capabilities for tolerance and love. Children also show these feelings. Only children who are distant from their parents always say, in a well behaved manner, how nice and kind their mommy and daddy are. Children who have a genuine relationship to their parents, occasionally curse their *dear* parents. They get furious with them and wish they would go to hell.[4]

Parents also have ambivalent feelings towards their children. Young mothers often admit shamefully that they have aggressive fantasies. They want to throw their screaming infant out the window or they feel a malicious pleasure when their child fails at something. Both children and parents have fantasies that can be aggressive or even mean. Parents often quickly repress such thoughts and the impulse to act is averted. The window is checked twice before we leave the children's room. The fact is that such thoughts and fantasies come up regularly and worry parents as well as children. The parent-child relationship is marked with the most divergent feelings.

Tensions and fights: the reality of the family

This psychological reality contradicts the ideal family picture that exists in our minds. When the ideal image is

---

[4] Editor's note: The German word used here is *Pfefferland*, which literally translated means *Pepperland*. English dictionaries translate this as Jericho. Most of us though who have a realistic view of our parents, do wish occasionally to send them to hell.

the harmonious, self-sufficient family, we repress other feelings and emotional states that emerge within a family. If we declare the family as the stronghold of contentment and happiness, it becomes difficult for family members to withstand it. Where do the demons go? It is impossible to live up to the family picture portrayed in advertisements or projected onto families in a community. The family idyll, where everything runs smoothly, does not exist. This family picture, leads to unrealistic expectations of family members of themselves and of parents for their children. A family does not guarantee happiness, and relationships are not free of the ugly sides of human personality. A family is a challenging community, rich with tension; a bold venture. We never know how a new family is going to develop when it is started. However the image of the harmonious family weighs on us and makes it difficult to endure everyday.

A family member's fears in the midst of a family are justified. If family members really are connected with one another, there also has to arise threatening feelings. And our children keep triggering new fears in us.

Children confront their parents with unfamiliar subjects, with leisure time activities whose meaning they do not understand or whose importance they judge badly. If a twelve year old daughter wants desperately to go to the *Guns n' Roses* concert with her friends, the parents might allow it wholeheartedly. They are reminded of their youth when they went to the great concerts of *The Rolling Stones*, *The Who*, *The Kinks* or Jimmy Hendrix. But what is their attitude with Game-Boy, video-games, or Futureland? Should we allow our children to dive into virtual reality war games? Children are growing up with games that are totally unfamiliar to adults. Often children stay home glaring into their screens on a beautiful, sunny day; a computer game has grabbed them. Children are influenced by outside groups, the Toys, Homies, Fly-Girls etc. A mother discovers a ninja star in the room of her fourteen year old son. "I'm only keeping it for a friend!" is his explanation. In other words we are confronted with challenges that are hard for us to judge. Leisure time activities arise that are unfamiliar, and we are not sure if they are having a brutalizing effect. On the one hand we do not want to close our eyes to new social tendencies, and on the other hand we fear for our children.

Today most children buy their own clothes. In the best situation, the father or mother have a voice in clothes decisions. Many children choose their clothing starting in kindergarten. Whether it is a Ramblers baseball hat, dressing all in black, or an oversized T-shirt, children have exact notions of what to wear and where to by it. Father or mother may, however, continue to discreetly have a background role as the big spender.

Language is a cause for concern. Adults believe to be witnessing a brutalizing of language. Of course one is tolerant as a rule, but what is one to do when one's children use words such as "bitch," "slut," and "fuck?" The personal tolerance melts away. We are alarmed, feel old, and reflect on what should be done against this deterioration of the language. Often we only notice crude language when we overhear our children talking with other children.

All these observations cause apprehensions. Is it true about the "terrible youth?" Maybe it is not only a distorted perspective of adults that dramatize dangers. Could it also be that children today matter of factly threaten to become degenerate? So it is imaginable that because of the contemporary seductions of drugs, alcohol, and the influences of videos, television, and movies, we really have to fear our children.

The *other* is also constellated where intimacy and closeness rule, and where we try to love. There are quarrels and clashes. Negative feelings merge with positive ones. How does this relate to our opening question? What position should a father or mother take towards these challenges. Parents and children are estranged from one another over and over again because of the fundamental ambivalence in a familial relationship and the fact that the younger generation embodies unknown tendencies and subjects. We only understand our children partially, are often excluded from their world, and are not capable of understanding their trends. A father or mother often experiences the feeling of failure because of this. Children take different roads than what we recommend. We cannot see the effects of our educational efforts.

Father and mother as archetype

In order to understand the meaning and role of the parent-child relationship, we have to step back. We have to view ourselves from outside and reflect on the deeper meanings of family. The parent-child relationship is not only personal. It also entails an archetypal aspect. This means that problems between parents and children are not always because of a mother's character or a father's actions, or a child's personal history. Sometimes dramas are instigated because of deeper needs.

The parent-child relationship represents an *ur*-pattern that is in us as a behavioral possibility. What happens in a family is not only acquired. Children and parents can follow paths that are already in our unconscious. We do not only engage our children with our personal psychology but also with archetypal forces that influence our reactions. Not only is the human being looked for in the mother or father, but also an impersonal dimension is searched for in the mother or father *themselves.*

On the one hand the archetypal shows itself in the way we want, as most parents do, to shelter, care for, and protect our children. On the other hand, it shows itself in our fears. In fact, most children do not simply look for a friend in the father but want to have *the* father. This is just as true as in school they do not want their teacher to be a friend but to be *the* teacher.

Mother and father represent opposite poles from an archetypal perspective. While children stand for change, curiosity, naiveté, and the spirit of adventure, it falls to the parents to be stable, protective, stubborn, and prohibitive. This should not be misunderstood. In their personal attitude parents can be open, progressive, and curious. Yet the deeper archetypal role they carry demands something different. It forces the parents to defend conservative values, to be "of yesterday," separate from the values and attitudes that they might actually practice. From their archetypal position, parents cannot be progressive and participate in their children's *zeitgeist.* The archetypal game demands that parents represent values, ideas, and attitudes of the past. What they say has to be "out" so that the children can find their place and have the feeling of discovering the world themselves. Children need the concerned father who thinks that what his son is doing is completely wrong as much as they need the enraged mother who furiously rips a toy pistol away from her child. In order for children to be able to enter into the world, to be naive, and behave without responsibility, parents have to represent out-dated positions. The concerned parental look gives the children the necessary space that they need to experiment with themselves and life. Father and mother have to *be* the *other* so that children may rebel in security and *be* of a different opinion. From an archetypal perspective parents and children are players in a drama where dynamics and positions are established, yet it is varied by different contents over and over again. This is a drama that repeats itself with each new generation. For that reason it is not the curriculum that is so important in education, but rather the attitude in which it is presented.

Fears can also be seen within this framework. Parents carry the existential apprehensions and fears of their children. Children delegate fears onto their parents so they can develop more freely. A thirteen year old boy told me that every time things were not going well in school, he would mention to his parents that he was probably going to be kicked out of school because he had flunked. Of course each time he did this, the parents were upset and worried. This way, the boy could play without worry. He had dumped his concerns and fears on mommy and daddy.

It is the parents' duty to worry because of this archetypal role. A father or mother must fear one's children. We have to fear that they are in the wrong circle of friends. We also have to repeatedly let our children make us insecure and concerned about them and their scary undertakings. The archetypal role as father or mother demands it.

Parents carry part of the shadow in the context of this relationship. They absorb the worry for the awful in the world. Children are under the impression that mother and father are old-fashioned, overly cautious, and see everything in black. On a deeper level however, they are pleased that mother and father take over this duty. When parents do not fulfill this duty, children often feel lost. For them, the wall is missing from which they can shove off and take into their hands the rudder of life. We always have to fear, and fear for, our children, because we constitute the *other*. Part of the violence of children in schools is due to the fact that schools and teachers do not take on these roles anymore. Teachers who only look for consensus and who want to discuss everything with their students do not give the students the opportunity to really be opposed to something. As a consequence violence can escalate until the longed for oppositional reaction takes place. Parents have the task of being the *other*, so that the child can place his or her fears, apprehensions, and cautions. The father who raises his eyebrows with concern when his daughter tells him that she was at the church fair, or the mother who vehemently insists that her son be home at nine o'clock, are needed. Only if parents fear their children and their development will children have the necessary protection for their growth. Parental fear gives the children a context in which they can be bold and let off steam.

CHAPTER SIX

NEW CHALLENGES FOR PARENTS AND SCHOOLS

The fascination of weapons

A further challenge that teachers and parents have to face are weapons. In some schools children show up with switchblades, gravity knives, butterfly knives, ninja-stars, baseball bats, clubs and even guns. At a school in a suburb of Berne two boys met on a field to settle a score. Each carried a baseball bat. The fight was short; soon both lay injured on the ground. Each had received a blow to the back of the head. According to the medical report, one of the boys barely survived. If the blow had struck a little bit higher, it would have been fatal.

Weapons in schools most often arrive in a creeping fashion. A particular weapon starts to fascinate the students. Certain boys then place a high value on possessing such a weapon. In one school throwing stars became popular. It started with one boy showing up with this weapon. Like a brush fire word spread through the entire school that a student was carrying this star and was threatening other children with it. Soon however the boy was not the only one. One week later other boys were also carrying this weapon. In order to be a "real boy," you had to have this weapon.

Mostly the origin of the weapon remains a mystery. "The father of a friend of mine bought this switchblade in Spain and gave it to me!" a twelve year old answered when I asked him where he got his knife. Different channels are used. If a particular weapon spreads around in school or in a neighborhood, children develop an incredible capacity for getting hold of one. They desperately look for ways to get their hands on a lock-knife or a club because of peer pressure. Weapons raise ones prestige in a group. However the danger of someone getting seriously hurt in fights increases with the presence of weapons in school.

> When I was in school I stuck a knife into another boy's chest. Thank God I hit him in the sternum, the bone that protects the chest. The knife only cut to the bone. There was blood everywhere but my friend from school was not seriously hurt. I stuck the knife into his chest simply because I had a knife. I did not hate him, did not even have a serious fight with him. I come from a stable, happy family. . . and was not being threatened by anyone. I was in love with my knife. It came from North Africa and had a green handle. It belonged to the aunt of a friend. She brought it back from Morocco.[1]

Ethnic mixing as a danger

The carrying of weapons becomes even more of a problem when there are differences of opinion among children about their use and meaning. Groups of children orient themselves according to their own guidelines. They are however heavily influenced by their cultural backgrounds. What meaning a certain weapon has, who

---

[1] This is from the memoirs of the English journalist Neal Ascherson, quoted from *The Independent*, 28 February 1993, 16.

carries it, and how it should be used, bases itself on the ideas developed by their ethnicity. Each popular group or religion advocates situations about what is permissible and what is not. The unconscious norms that are represented by the given societies or groups, can contradict one another.

An Albanian child appeared in school with a handgun. During recess he waved it around and pointed it at his friends. Fear and terror spread throughout the playground. The teacher took the weapon from the boy, and talked to the father, pointing out his son's behavior to him. Indignant, the father rejected all reproaches. To take away his son's handgun was equivalent to castrating him! In his country it is absolutely the custom that boys after a certain age carry handguns.

If cultures mix, then different ways of behaving clash. While it is common in one country that each boy carries knife on him, in another culture the most that is allowed is water pistols. Before in northern European countries carrying any kind of knife was prohibited, yet in Switzerland, a "real boy" owns a pocketknife. Insecurities emerge where different cultural patterns meet. When no traditional cultural agreements over the carrying of weapons are valid, it can happen that children and teenagers yield to the fascination of weapons, and in this way try to compensate for feelings of insecurity that occur in an ethnically mixed territory.

In certain regions and schools, children and teenagers try to assert themselves by grouping together; Yugoslav Power, Turkish Tigers, or Latinos. Socially and culturally disoriented children and teenagers look for a feeling of security by looking back to their cultural roots. They try to overcome their subjectively insecure surroundings by parading their ethnic symbols. If an ethnic group defines itself through certain weapons, the consequences are fatal. As we know from the United States, it can lead to utterly violent, armed disputes. If a higher ideal about the ownership of weapons is lacking, different subgroups will set the norm.

Defenseless girls, brutal boys?

Apparently boys lean more towards violence than girls do. It is almost always boys who are the culprits when it comes to destruction, threats and fights. Girls have a lesser tendency to open, brutal violence. They hold back more and are more sociable. Can girls be violent, or are they mainly victims?

When it comes to frequency, violent acts by boys clearly dominate. Still there are cases of female violence. This violence differs in quality from that of the boys'. When girls are aggressive, it is expressed in a different manner. Basically it holds true that girls have a much lower level of tolerance when it comes to violence. What two boys may consider as a harmless scuffle, girls experience as an ugly fight. Their sense of what still may be acceptable differs from that of the boys. This different threshold leads girls to constantly feel threatened and under attack. Meanwhile the boys are astonished and under the impression that these "biddies" are obviously hysterical.

Further noticeable with girls is their fine-tuned aggression. Violence is aimed directly at the weaknesses in the personality of the opponent. The fight is directed at the other's personality. Female aggression is often more personal, direct, and in a certain sense, more effective.

In a fifth grade a rather awkward, introverted boy tried to get his friends' attention. He was rejected by the other kids because of his looks and his interest in mineralogy. He was not "in." The boy tried to hook up with a group of girls hoping at least to make some good girl friends. The girls however made themselves scarce. So he was happily surprised when he received a carefully wrapped audio tape for his birthday. Excitedly he opened the package and put the tape into the player full of expectations. Instead of music or a story, he heard ugly insults. "Your looks make us want to throw up. Please grow back into the womb, then abort. You can't even be used as a cunt lick."

Girls also seem more capable of quickly changing their face. A girl spits in another's face or steals a notebook. Two seconds later she faces the teacher with the sweetest, most harmless expression. The aggressive behavior of girls is often less obvious. Boys tend to lean more towards open, blunt aggression, and consequently get caught more.

In gang or group violence girls often participate in the background. They admire the actions of their boy friends, egg them on, and get them agitated. They distribute their blessings according to the behavior of the boys. It is rare that girls let themselves be pulled into direct violence.

A high school class went through several teacher changes. The time in which a teacher could stand teaching the class became shorter and shorter. Finally a substitute arrived who decided to be tough. His attention focused particularly on an aggressive group of boys. The entire class decided to take some action against this hated teacher. Four girls declared themselves willing to wait for him on the street, and if necessary, steal his briefcase. They actually followed through with the attack. The teacher was so upset, he handed in his resignation.

Such muggings are rare. What was striking with this group of girls was that they were all very attractive, fashionably dressed, young women. They looked far from being violent.

Once in awhile it happens that girls take over, especially in the age group between eleven and thirteen. It is well known that girls are physically stronger than boys at that age. They are aware of their superiority and take advantage of it. They start to define themselves differently socially. In one class this behavior was triggered through a self-defense class that parents had sent their daughters to attend. They used their defense tactics in the class and quickly became a great threat to the boys. The girls did however not only use their new capabilities to defend themselves, but also acted as a gang. They carried out kissing raids on younger, good-looking boys, threatened classmates and forced them to kiss their shoes. What was interesting was the reaction of the boys. When they realized that the girls were more powerful, they regressed completely. They acted just like young children, cried easily and lost all courage. Their feeling of self-worth broke down.

Girls can also be aggressive and mean towards teachers they do not like. Often they know exactly which subject to pick in order to make the teacher insecure. A teacher received a threatening letter from two difficult girls in which they accused her of being a lesbian and of having sexually abused them. The girls threatened to denounce her to the school administration and school board if she did not disappear immediately. These girls understood how to take advantage of the omnipresent theme of sexual abuse.

Dismay and Anger: reactions of parents and teachers

When your own son or daughter gets tormented, excluded, threatened, or beat up at school, you are deeply upset as a parent. Feelings of fury emerge when you notice that your daughter is loosing enthusiasm for classes and cannot fall asleep at night because of incidents happening in the school yard or classroom. We wish that our children will have a nice time at school, gain knowledge and skills, and we are upset when we notice that the school is turning into a horror for our children. School should be a place where children are introduced to positive aspects of human existence, not institutions where fear and terror are spread. If their child gets tormented in school, parents' are accordingly furious. Many children keep these incidents to themselves in fear of giving away their peers or losing their independence.

Three thirteen year old boys happened to meet an eight year old boy from their school in front of the school at the gym pole.[2] They made it clear to him that he was not supposed to be there. When he tried to run away, they grabbed him, and tossed him around. They made him stand in the middle of the school yard near the gym pole and pull down his pants. Then they made him manipulate his member. They told him to masturbate in public. The incident was observed by a woman neighbor who did not intervene.

However the next day the neighbor reported the incident to the school administration. They tried to identify the victim. According to the neighbor's description, the little boy had run away sobbing in total despair when the older boys finally let him go. Only a week later could the victim be identified. The eight year old boy had not told his parents about what happened. The parents said he came home from school grumpy that day, immediately

---

[2] Translator's note: The gym pole, *Turnstangen* in German, is a tall, climbing pole located in all school yards in Switzerland. Gym classes are held around it in good weather, and a part of gym class involves having the children climb the pole.

went to his room, and told his parents he was not hungry. The father said he also was in a strange mood the following days. The incident in that school yard was too embarrassing for the boy and had injured his self-esteem too deeply in order for him to tell his teacher or parents.

As a parent you are emotionally affected when your child suffers. You look intensely for an explanation for such incidents. How could this happen? What are the causes? Where are the culprits? During this often prolonged ordeal, parents develop explanations and theories. Depending on their philosophical outlook and ideology, they try to understand the fights, abuses and threats. They fall back to their system of references in order to be able to assimilate the incidents in an intelligent way.

Many parents are under the impression that the fault lies in the school. The teachers should be ready to take more severe actions and punish the culprits. If Beat and Marcus were expelled from school, the problem would be solved. Or if the teacher was consistent the incidents would decrease. Others go in the opposite direction. They say the lessons are too strict. The children need more space and understanding.

Often the parents' complaints refer to the class's composition. They say the percentage of foreigners is too high or the percentage of girls too low. The community can also be criticized. In their desperate search for a cause, they say, "It is obvious that things cannot go well if so many children from Hirzbach[3] are in the school. Afterall, mostly foreigners and single mothers live in this neighborhood."

The parents' explanations are varied and partially bizarre, but they do often contain a grain of truth. They

---

[3] Editor's note: This is a poorer neighborhood in Zürich.

vehemently defend their explanations because they are upset. Understandably parents want things for their children to improve and therefore request that measures be taken that agree with their ideas. Yet often their child is exempted from such measures. They want drastic steps to be taken in school—as soon as an incident occurs the student should be sent home—except when it involves their child.

The situation is similarly difficult for the teacher. Teaching becomes hard if violence escalates in the class, or if there is an aggressive atmosphere and incidents keep on occurring. On the one hand the teacher gets sick of teaching when they can only open the classroom door after saying a silent prayer. On the other hand the teacher experiences the incidents as personal failures. Teaching becomes an ordeal, and many teachers become allergic to their class under these circumstances. They expect the worst before they arrive at their classroom. They greet the class in a bad mood. The teacher barks, "Where are your notebooks? You are supposed to have them on your desk!" Another teacher snaps at a class which he has not seen in four days. Instead of a greeting, the class is met with accusations. If the lesson is experienced as a personal failure, it can turn into a personal crisis. Older teachers feel they no longer can reach the new generation. The children are alien to them and seem controlled by a malignant spirit. Inside they say good-bye to teaching. They count the month or weeks to the day when classes end. The hours are endured and the personal input is limited to causing the least amount of damage. If classes are experienced as personal failures, the impact on private life should not be excluded. Depression can set in caused by a lack of meaningful work.

Younger teachers often feel let down by their courses in teacher training. They are disappointed that the students do not behave according to their teaching ideals. They entered the teaching profession with the belief that they could motivate and inspire children in their class with good teaching. If they find that their openness and willingness towards dialogue and their positive attitudes are not rewarded, a deep disappointment comes over them. They think "What is the matter with these kids? Why are they not participating in this project in which I have invested so much time?" Younger teachers often face their classes perplexed and without understanding. They question "How is it possible that a boy is beaten up by two friends for just wearing red sneakers after we spent two hours talking about conflict resolution?"

Just like parents, teachers also look for causes of violence and plausible explanations. Yet from their perspective it is not the school or classes that are responsible for the children's violence, but the family or free-time activities. Many teachers emphasize that the children arrive at school all wound up, tense, tired and potentially aggressive. From the teacher's perspective, the children are exposed to an array of influences that encourage violent behavior; too much watching of television, crowded living conditions, a repressive upbringing or a lack of supervision. If a ten year old is allowed to roam around the city every night, do not be surprised if she is irritable at school. If a father does not dare oppose his thirteen year old son who announces that he does not plan to help with chores in any way, and is going to continue to come and go as it pleases him, similar difficulties can be expected at school.

Depending on the neighborhood, the teachers connect violent behavior and the "scene" in the area. It is reasoned

Depending on the neighborhood, the teachers connect violent behavior and the "scene" in the area. It is reasoned that the students are violent because of the influence of the outside homeboy and toy scene. Viewed from this perspective, the students would be good if only the homies were not causing trouble. Their students and school are viewed as victims of outside influences.

In a large Bern school it became apparent that outside teenagers kept on hanging around the school. Because it was a very large school, teenagers from the outside could not be distinguished from teenagers who were supposed to be there. During the crisis intervention session, it was discovered that these outside teenagers would beat up students for the small sum of two to five francs.[4]

Members of such gangs can also become dangerous to the teachers. In a St. Gallen school, an uninvited member of a gang entered a gym where a teacher was teaching a class. The outsider confronted a student with whom he had a score to settle. When the teacher intervened and demanded that the student leave the gym, the outsider attacked the teacher. The teacher defended himself, and it turned into a fight. The teacher told his students to call security. The class however did nothing (probably because they first wanted to see who would win).

Schools usually attribute the causes of violence exclusively to external factors. Therefore teachers often dismiss parental complaints. They demand that changes be made in the upbringing, in the environment, or in the free-time activities of the children and teenagers.

The reciprocal mental externalization of the factors that cause violence leads to inaction. If parents or teachers only acknowledge the external factors of violence, the

---

[4] Editor's note: This amount in Swiss francs represents about two to four U. S. dollars.

danger persists that nothing will be done against the violence. Teachers put demands on the parents, parents accuse the teaching staff and both attack the media. Each
one blames the other. This entails the danger of not recognizing ones own part in the violence.

The hidden side of violence

According to a psychoanalytical picture of humanity,
we do not only have noble sides in us but also destructive
tendencies. Humans have shadows that consist of repressed and unacceptable psychic material. Consciously
we reject violence. Yet it emerges in our unconscious or
Shadow personality. It is difficult to recognize your
Shadow. We find it easier to project elements of this
Shadow onto the outside. Since we have reject the incom-
patible contents of our unconscious with our consciousness, we transfer them into our surroundings. If a teenager insists he is innocent and that he is not at fault for a
fight but was provoked, he has projected his violent aspect. Violent incidents should always also remind us of
our own potential for violence.

The confrontation with the Shadow is one of the most
difficult psychological challenges that exists. Since we
want to see ourselves as wonderful and perfect, it is difficult for us to recognize our violent sides.

A further difficulty is found in the search for solutions. We always lapse into the naive belief that there are
solutions that will eliminate violence from the world forever. Since however violence belongs to the human
Shadow, it will keep on reappearing. We cannot surgi-
cally remove violent tendencies out of the human being.

If we want to do something against violence, we have
to except it as an internal possibility. The problem of
violence cannot be solved, but we have to take on violence as a constant challenge and keep on inventing new

measures against it so that it does not take over and destroy us. We have to except Mr. Hyde as a companion of
our existence, so we can be Dr. Jekyll.

In relation to school this means that violence can only
be curbed if all parties actively participate and renounce
blame. The basis of crisis intervention is the mutual confrontation of this Shadow subject. Violence is understood
as a common civilizing challenge where over and over
again institutions, rules, ideals and rituals have to be developed.

A teacher's double role

It is difficult for a teacher to react correctly to violence. The idea of the peaceful, wonderful, harmonious
class where the teacher is always in control and is loved
has to be let go. A teacher today has to accept that over
and over again chaos prevention has to be practiced. On a
classroom level the teacher is assigned a double function:
on the one hand to be a teacher and sponsor of the children's development, and on the other to be a head gang
leader. On an individual basis a teacher tries to engage the
children, recognize their problems and difficulties, and
build a relationship with them. Yet in front of the class a
teacher has to be a gang leader. In order to prevent
Shadow forces from constellating and taking over, the
teacher has to be an archetypal counter-pole, representing
the super ego that rejects violence. As the head gang
leader, a teacher is less interested in the individual child,
and more in the subject and dynamics of the group. As
the gang leader, the teacher sets the guidelines.

This means though that over and over again a teacher
has to withstand alienation. Students do not want to understand a teacher's instructions. They will put up resistance, complain and moan. To stand this kind of rejection is often difficult for a teacher. On a deeper level

however children need to have a gang leader. They want someone in the class who lays down the law even if they do not follow it. Only if they are clear about the teacher's position when there arises a counter-pole to the teacher, can they find their own position, rituals, and mobilize themselves against violence and aggression.

The necessity of orally transmitted school ideals

On the level of the school, there needs to be a counter-culture to violence. Only if the teaching staff develops a mutual will, can it prevent violence from taking over. This counter culture needs a consensus on what will be tolerated in the school and what will not. To what extent are fights allowed? What is the reaction going to be if a student plays hooky or appears with a weapon at school? As described in the chapter on school culture, common teaching ideals are needed so that students can orient themselves. These ideals must contain statements regarding violence and aggression. It must be made clear what is considered healthy aggression and at what point violence begins.

Furthermore it is important that the teaching staff believe in these collective teaching principals and statements; not just follow them on paper. Unfortunately many schools limit their philosophical consensus to rules. Soon however the rules turn into a way of getting away from implementing a school's ideals.

Instead of developing a mission statement that can be quoted at any time and made comprehensible to the students, teachers refer to a dead piece of paper. In many schools its seems that rules relieve the teacher from the duty of being effective throughout the whole school.

A rule cannot replace a collective teaching culture. What is written on a piece of paper especially does not effect young children since they are not accustomed to centering themselves on what is written. Therefore the teaching principals have to be given to the children orally. They have to contain images and expressions that make an impression and are not soon forgotten. Young children center themselves on what the teacher says spontaneously and not according to dead paragraphs.

In order to develop such a common set of beliefs, the teaching staff has to sit together and take the time to develop a consensus. Often intensive discussions are necessary, possibly with the help of a facilitator, until general agreement is found. Up to what point are fights among students to be tolerated? What punishments are the teaching staff to impose? What happens when property is damaged? Such topics should be discussed in the framework of setting up orally transmitted ideals.

Naturally, the children will not abide by these rules. Yet the teacher's view is of psychological significance. The ideals will present a counter-pole to the children's opinions. They will help the children develop their own positions. Of course students will not accept the ideas of the teaching staff, but through a discourse with these ideals, they will develop their own attitudes.

For example in a school in Thurgau, bicycles were being vandalized over and over again. Brake cables were cut, tires slit and wheels taken off. After two more incidents happened, the teaching staff reacted with physical punishment. They announced that any student caught vandalizing bicycles would have to help the janitor clean an entire afternoon. The teachers agreed that they would without exception apply the same punishment and not allow for any exceptions. The students were actually impressed with the teachers' unified will. The vandalizing stopped. The only thing that continued was the deflating of tires. The students had not simply adopted the teachers' policy, but thanks to the teaching staff's firm attitude, they had found their own solution to the problem. The students took it upon themselves to punish those students who went further than was allowed. The teachers' collective resolve helped the students to more or less handle the problem. A certain amount of violence was permitted, but the students knew how far to go. In this last situation it was a question of provoking a reaction from the students. In a crisis intervention situation, children should be helped to develop ways of dealing with problems.

A further thing that has been very helpful in the case of violent incidents in school is publicity. If incidents occur in the school or in the immediate vicinity, all teachers and students should be informed. The entire school should know what happened and how it came about. The names of the participating students should be made public. Through these measures social controls within the school are strengthened. It is important that violent incidents do not occur privately but become public within the framework of the school. In this way it is made clear to those students involved that they exclude themselves from the community through their actions and that certain violent acts are not tolerated. However making public violent students' names and a description of the incidents, also serves the purpose of sensitizing the rest of the school as to where, according to the teachers and parents, the line should be drawn.

Under no circumstances, of course, are the publishing of the names to be the only measures taken. Parallel to this there has to be talks with the violent students. And they should have the opportunity to redefine themselves within the framework of school.

CHAPTER SEVEN

SCHOOL CULTURE AS A PEDAGOGIC CHALLENGE

I like the work with the children very much. However the atmosphere in the teachers' lounge irritates me. There is talk about the gym's floor coverings, school trips, parents' negligence, or the weekend. There is not one word about problems with one's class! Apparently all my colleagues handle their profession's challenges with ease!

This statement comes from an elementary school teacher who was battling several problems in her job. She had to contend with a difficult group of boys, reproachful parents, and classes that kept on sliding into chaos. She maintained her composure in the teachers' lounge—as a new teacher she did not want to become a problem case, so she kept quiet. In the school she never felt part of it. Behind closed doors, the children drive her to total desperation. All the while she is nonchalant to the outside. The "intimate atmosphere, the classroom" no matter how desperate, is not allowed to be looked in on.

Pedagogy concentrates on this area, whereas the school buildings and grounds are regarded as the janitors' territory, their world. While "working with colleagues" is recommended and praised, it is often limited to the exchange of lesson plans or to organizing a field day. Personal instruction stays private, split off from the rest of the school.

Every profession is based on ideas of how it should be performed. Ideals serve as a point of orientation and define the field of operation. A hotel owner either sees himself responsible for the well-being of his guests or limits his efforts to changing beds and making breakfast. The focus of the work is defined by the ideal in the profession. The professional ideal directs the professional efforts and defines the place where the work will occur. For the teacher, class work is central. The sounding of the school bell becomes the prelude to a personal mission in front of a group of children, the lesson a medium of influence, and the subject matter, a legitimization. According to this ideal the efforts of the teacher concentrate on didactic questions, involvement with individual children, working with parents, and a teaching style. A good teacher can give stimulating lessons and excite students to learn. As correct as this ideal might be, it only covers part of the reality of the teaching profession and does not address the changing demands of schools.

The school—carrier of projections

Viewed from the outside, a different perspective opens up. The school is seen and judged as a whole. "In the Aebiacker school the teachers are very strict. In the Rüeschegg school there is a liberal or free-style, so that things are almost chaotic." The village or neighborhood gossip gives characteristics to the schools. Not only does the individual teacher become the focus of interest, but the school takes on its own character (*Gestalt*). Schools do not only serve to accommodate different school classes but carry meaning as an institution. The teaching staff is scrutinized for its attitudinal values, because school has an important place in the life of a community. With all seeing eyes the surrounding community watches the school for signs through which the attitudes of the teaching staff can be recognized. The community registers all information coming out of a school and weaves an image of the school. A custodian who wants to have the school empty twenty minutes after school ends, or a teacher who always drives in just two minutes before class, sends out messages to the community. If the Special Education's bicycle stand is the only one that is covered in the rain, it is clearly noted and leads to conclusions about the teachers' attitudes. This remains true even when individual teachers are confronted with the situation. Schools are not neutral "things;" they are observed for meanings. They are symbols for parents and people, symbols which crystallize the community's social tendencies, positions, and attitudes.

Also, precise fantasies about life in the school circulate among children. Different subcultures, that can either be attractive or frightening, are identified in the school. "All the nerds are in the Dössegger school." Entering a school means confronting this children's world, that defines rituals, steers fashions, influences manners, and often determines a teacher's school career.

The fantasies about the schools can be true or false, but in every case they carry the qualities of a collective transference. The school is filled with its own concerns, problems and wishes and serves as symbol of and for the community spirit. The contents projected onto the school express the relation between the state or local municipality on the one hand, and children and adults on the other. Immigrants vent the expectations, problems and hopes which they carry with them into our culture.

School shows them our community's willingness to integrate foreigners. Can my children assimilate themselves here? For Swiss parents, however, school often is the object to which they attach their critical attitudes towards society in general, or from which they expect a clear stance against today's trends. The challenges that a community or neighborhood is faced with crystallize in school. The surroundings functionalizes the school according to its psychology. The collective soul that marks a community or neighborhood are expressed in the way a school is perceived by its surroundings.

These communal meanings of the school often, unfortunately, stand in crass contrast with the staff's self definition of its work. We rarely recognize this psychological environment in which a school is embedded. The teacher can afford to retreat into his or her four walls because he or she is not directly dependent on the surroundings, and the children have to attend classes by law. When however the teaching staff view themselves exclusively as schedule soldiers, they miss the opportunity of making an impact on the surroundings as an institution and forming the school's image. The psychological desire of the children, the parents and some teachers to give meaning to the concept of school is not being satisfied.

Schools are not only learning institutions. They can be mediators of a pedagogic message which gives direction to the staff, the children and the community. Only when the entire school comes together and works on—as already called for by the pedagogue Herbart—a unified school life, and tries to articulate common pedagogic positions, there is hope that the school can live up to its communal significance.

School is a pedagogic unity that demands intensive cooperation amongst teachers. The personal pedagogic attitude, the difficulties in teaching, and in contact with parents are no private matter, but are always also a concern of the entire school. Embarrassments in class should be talked about not only within a private setting or, if need be, under personal supervision, but should be seen as a pedagogic challenge to the entire team of teachers.

School culture can help children participate in a school that offers more than subject matter, discipline and class egoism. School can become a piece of home. This is of particular significance in urban areas or anonymous suburbs with a large foreigner population. The nurturing of a school culture belongs also among the preventive measures for coping with drugs, degeneration and violence.

The reality of many schools is hardly ideal. The school building is rarely fantasized about, the teaching staff as a relational group figures least in teaching, internal conflicts are evaded, and teacher conferences are regarded as additional assignments. Astoundingly, it is still possible for a teacher to get out of continuing education conferences, even if organized by an active teacher group or a school board of education, without hurting their careers. This is done on the grounds that "there are no problems in my class," or "I would rather take part in a computer course during that time" or " I have to do research for my school field trip."[1] These behavioral patterns of teachers show that the idea "school culture" at most carries merely a rhetorical meaning. Often the school is not looked at as a workplace that demands a fuller presence beyond teaching hours, but just as a place to fill in a schedule. There is little time for the interior design of the school building,

---

[1] Editor's note: This is called a *Klassenlager*. Every year Swiss classes go away and stay in youth hostels for a week or a couple of nights depending on the grade the children are in.

the hallways, the recreational areas, for relationship between teachers and for events after school. In extreme
cases interest is reduced to muffins and coffee in the
teacher's lounge, while the expectations of the milieu and
events on the playground are tuned out.

An alive school culture as an opportunity

One of the central challenges facing schools today is to
foster an active school culture. So that "school culture"
does not remain empty words and schools can fulfill their
communal purpose and teachers find support in their
work by the team, practical efforts in different areas are
necessary. Above all, the teaching staff must work out
teaching guidelines for the entire school. How is violence
responded to in our school? What significance is given to
grades? How do we try to integrate foreign children?
Guidelines are needed that can be understood by the
community and by children. Pedagogic principles that
children and parents can orient themselves after—against
which they can rebel or with which they can identify—
ought not be reduced to rules and regulations on a piece
of paper lying in a drawer, or posted for children as ab-
stract house rules. The principles rather should describe
ideas that the teaching staff takes to heart and that can be
quoted spontaneously by children and parents alike.

School culture also contains conflict consciousness.
How is fighting being done in school? Are there open
disputes among the teaching staff or do they give way to
intrigues? Questions of teamwork arise: how are new
colleagues introduced? Does a new colleague first have to
"walk into the fire" and understand that children are different from what the naive pedagogues lectured about in
college, before he or she is more or less accepted? Or will
the teaching staff support a new colleague from the start?

Further thought has to be given to dramas in the playground. School yard supervision does not mean standing watch at the doorway, waiting until something happens somewhere. Instead during recess supervision time you should fantasize about the happenings on the playground. What positions, hierarchies, typical and problematic behaviors can be detected among the hordes of children? Recess supervision is an opportunity to study the children's subculture.

Furthermore it is important that the teaching staff agrees on the meaning of punishment. Should there be punishment? What is it to be? Can the teachers mutually support each other? What should be the reaction if two boys fight in the hallway?

Then, work with parents becomes very significant. Instead of letting yourself be out foxed by the parents, nodding your head in understanding when a mother complains about a colleague's work, or instead of lamenting that parents today no longer want to bring up their children, it is a question of developing a common strategy with other teachers that takes hold of the whole class. How is the school seen by the parents? What expectations are being put on to the school? What is the reaction going to be if a child cuts school, or if parents meddle with the class lessons?

Apart from the educational position conveyed to the outside world, a search for answers to contemporary educational challenges also belongs to school culture. Should ten year old boys and girls be allowed to have pajama parties? How much free-time activity can an eight year old handle? May I buy my son a baseball bat? Particularly for single mothers and fathers as well as immigrants, it can be of great help if they know with the school's policy on these questions. Guiding principles

cannot be announced *ex cathedra* but only in dialogue
with the community, so that regional peculiarities are
taken into account. While one neighborhood discusses
how many times the movies should be frequented, parents in another district do not know how to deal with the
youth scene in the local mall. A school culture guides
children and parents so they do not have to feel out each
teacher's pedagogic position, but know which common
values the school upholds.

A vivacious school culture includes events that go beyond school: parties, celebrations, or projects in which
the entire school participates and which the students help
organize. It is even possible to have weekly student conferences where the students raise concerns and discuss
problems. Such events convey to the students the feeling
of participating in something larger. These events increase
the chances that children will develop a sense for higher
structures and become participants in the community. If,
at such a weekly meeting, students hear from the feared
school bully that she also is anxious and, in addition, feels
excluded by others, they might see her differently and
forestall her aggressive defensiveness.

Another part of school culture asks from the teaching
staff reflections on the subcultures that establish themselves in schools. Most students are not aware of what
their teachers think of the behavior and fashions that they
try. Should martial arts be practiced on the playground?
Are switchblades permitted at school? It helps children if
they have a notion of the attitude of the school so that
they can develop counter forces to questionable practices
taking place on the school premises. If in a school, it becomes common to use crude sexual words to insult one
another, there is a demand for a counter voice that represents the attitude of the school. The children's world

expects a strong position from the school so that an independent moral attitude can be found and the direction of the group is not set by problem, hyper-aggressive children.

School culture also means that a teaching staff reflects on itself and makes a theme out of the school's dynamic. A statement like, "I have no problem with my class and have everything under total control," carries a different meaning if at the same time students from this class terrorize the playground. It is a question of reflecting on the role of one's own class within the school. Maybe first there has to be a paradigm shift, a mental leap, so that teachers do not just see themselves as solitary fighters, but tied into a group that gives the school guidance, works on the internal climate, and effects the community.

It is questionable whether our schools can develop enough strength from within for a common school culture. Mostly the personalities of the teachers are too different and their working methods too individualized to find a common denominator. The prerequisite conditions for a dynamic school culture, therefore, is a person in charge who represents the school to the outside world and who sees herself or himself responsible for the school's teaching premises. School culture requires a superintendent with special authority, that over and over again broaches the subject of the school culture and who serves as the person the educational directors can address regarding all school projects.

As a final thought, a further advantageous condition for a positive school culture is the size of the school. From experience it is far easier for smaller schools to agree upon ideals than it is for larger anonymous school factories.

CHAPTER EIGHT

CRISIS INTERVENTION

I *n the following pages, a model of the crisis intervention program used for violent school classes by the Board of Education of the Canton of Bern (Switzerland) is introduced. The program was developed by the author, yet it has been perfected and implemented over the last several years with the help of psychologists and psychology students who work for the Bern Board of Education on an hourly basis as group therapists for children.*

To begin

A teacher calls up the board of education all upset.

> I can't stand this any longer! My class is slipping away from me! The mood among the students is miserable! On top of it an ugly incident occurred last week. A girl was pushed out of the first floor window, and she broke her arm. The parents are complaining to the school administrators. I'm totally desperate!

Such a cry for help can be the start of a crisis intervention. A teacher has reached the end of her rope. She does not dare get in front of the class anymore. She has to stand and watch the students spit into each other's faces, hit each other in the stomach, and gleefully destroy school property.

The teacher has the sense of having tried everything. First, she appealed to the students' good sense and, during several conversations, asked for their insights. When this did not work, she tried stricter measures. She issued warnings and threatened punishments. She did, however, lack the strength to follow up on her punishments. Now the students are dancing around right in front of the teacher's nose. While she is teaching the class, a student zips around the desks on his skate board. She is barely tolerated as a decorative figure in the classroom and has no influence over the students. After the incident of the broken arm, a parents' group began demanding measures be taken in the school; some parents wanted her fired.

This is a flagrant case. How could it get to this point? Talks with the school administrators and the teacher show that this class has had many teacher changes. Within a two year period they had six different teachers. Some of these teachers were not very good, yet some were competent. This frequent change in teachers resulted in the class not wanting to listen to a teacher anymore, assuming that the teacher would be leaving soon. The quicker they got rid of the teacher, the better. By driving away the teachers, the class built a negative identity, which made it feel strong and gave it a group sense. The goal of this class was to take out the teachers.

In her defense, the teacher had just received her diploma, and this fifth grade was her first job. Enthusiastic about students setting their own goals, groups working together and individualistic teaching, she decentralized the arrangement of the classroom, and encouraged the students to work autonomously. She presented herself as a guide to learning. It was against her grain to be authoritative. She viewed herself as an older friend. The class found this teacher sympathetic, yet did not want to get close to her because they feared loosing her. The fear of separation led to the class's lack of co-operation. The class was seized by the dynamics from which it could not get free. Teacher and class were both trapped.

The broken arm incident was the last straw. Unfortunately the accident occurred during class which caused the members of the community to shake their heads in disbelief. The teacher wanted the class to do some project, so she had divided up the classroom. One group was working behind a wall of closets. Instead of working on the project, they had decided to climb out the window. When a girl hesitated, the boys pushed her out.

From this situation came the cry for help for crisis intervention. The long history of the class and their teacher is typical in this case. The violent incident must be viewed in connection with the history, teacher's personality and the dynamics of the class. Violence in school often does not just occur out of the blue but is the result of an unfortunate development caused by several factors.

Most interventions are brought by the teacher. Difficulties in asserting one's will, incidents of violence, tensions with parents, or other incidents in the school, cause teachers to seek help from outside. The start of a crisis intervention begins with a teacher feeling not in control anymore or that the students are too violent. Objective criteria is not used as a basis for a crisis intervention. The decision usually lies with a teacher.

Often however crisis interventions can be initiated by school administrators. They can request an intervention if there is an increase of complaints from parents over incidents in school, if there is a negative school report, or if there are other signs indicating that an orderly school is no longer in place. First of all they have to get the agreement of the teacher in question. An intervention only has a chance of succeeding if the teacher actively participates. If the consensus is there, the school administrators, together with the teacher, can begin an intervention.

More rarely, interventions are called for by parents' groups. Parents get active when the administrators or teaching staff try to make the troubles seem harmless and do not take their concerns seriously. If the parents ask for an intervention, this can be taken as a sign that the dialogue between teachers and parents is not working. Teachers can barricade themselves behind formalism, refuse to inform the parents correctly about the class, or take few disciplinary measures against individual students. Such behavior is closely monitored by the parents and often cause problems to get bigger. Then a situation is created where both sides hurl accusations at each other.

Stopping the blame

Whether the school administrators, the teachers, or a parents' group seek help is unimportant. No matter who calls for the intervention, the procedures are always the same. No orders are permitted to be given from either the teaching staff, the school administrators or parents, because violence is a mutual challenge. All parties are called to contribute to overcoming the problem, to refrain from casting blame, and to focus on possible solutions. The issue is not to identify difficult students and possibly expel them, or to help out a teacher, but to draw on the school's internal resources to calm down the situation. Crisis intervention is not a surgical procedure which cuts the diseased part out. It is an attempt, initiated from outside, to mobilize forces in parents, teachers, administrators and students. The question is not who carries the blame for the problems, but what can each person do in their own way to solve the problems.

To put aside guilt is often not easy because we are all too ready to look for, and find, the guilty. A headmaster declared that, "In our school it is the homeboys from the outside who are ruining the school." A group of parents complained, "This teacher has been promising the students for years to take them on a one week school trip, and this unfulfilled promise is the cause of the class's rebellion!" Or, "We know two boys are the leaders. They need to be expelled from school, then everything will be fine." External groups have an effect on the school, individual, aggressive children stand out, and teachers cause violent outbreaks with insensitive or stupid actions.

The connections seen by parents, school administrators or teachers often contain truth. In the framework of a crisis intervention, however, we do not focus on these connections and causes, but only look at them as a secondary point. The stasis caused by mutual blaming has to be overcome.

The all-or-nothing principle

"All-or-nothing" is the next principle of a crisis intervention. The "all" refers to the seven points of an intervention. These are: conferences with the teachers, school visits, parents' night, mythodramas, teacher mentoring, a final intervention session, and a closing evening. All seven points have to be accepted by the participating parties. Individual points are not to be removed from the intervention package and carried out by themselves. For example it is not possible to only have a parents' information evening or to just work with a class. If a crisis intervention takes place, all parties involved, teachers, administrators and parents, have to support all seven points. According to the all-or-nothing principle, an intervention only begins if the entire package is accepted.

The all-or-nothing principle is important because without it one of the parties can easily avoid responsibilities. For example the administrators might organize an informational evening where they complain about the influence of the media and youth culture, at the same time refusing to look at incidents occurring in their school. Or a teacher might want us to work with his class and carry out the mythodrama but is not willing to reflect on the part he plays during our teacher conferences.

If only one point of the crisis intervention is executed, there is the danger that one party's role is not recognized. This will continue to induce violence. A crisis intervention only has a chance to succeed when all seven points are followed.

In the following pages, these seven points will be described. For each point its goal will be made clear, and then I will illustrate it with some of my experiences. Basically this seven point program is most useful in primary school from 2nd to 6th grade. The program is slightly changed for high schools or middle schools.

The teacher conferences

The first point in a crisis intervention is the conference with the teacher. The goal of this conference is to help the teacher reflect on his or her work and to re-evaluate his or her teaching approach. In a discussion with the head of the crisis intervention team, the teacher should present his or her record in the school, a view of the class, a perception of difficult students, the work with the parents, and his or her fundamental attitude towards school. Everything that a teacher brings into the classroom has to be looked at in this discussion. The teacher should talk about his or her personal history. It often happens that a teacher comes to a class burdened with a long history. It became clear with one teacher that an authority problem was blocking him. As a son of an authoritative father, he had at an early age rebelled against rules. Bureaucrats always caused him difficulty, whether school or government officials. He avoided military service and fought with his father. This authority complex also effected his teaching. He was not capable of presenting himself as an authority figure. His personal background prevented him from asserting himself or getting his way when it came to violence. He tried to solve the problem of violence with new ideas, talk or concern, but failed to inform his students about his attitude. This background had to be thought about so that he could find a new start in the classroom.

With one teacher it became apparent, during the teacher conference, that she tried to fend off her depression through strict and authoritative behavior. As the daughter of a psychotic mother and an alcoholic father, she was only able to develop a personality thanks to immense personal efforts. She had to be strict with herself so that her Shadow sides would not break through. This background resulted in her overreacting to violence in her class. She meted out harsh punishments and rejected those students who were violent. This was counterproductive for the class as the students noticed that their teacher was dealing with a personal problem. The class rebelled. Certain students suffered under the atmosphere. One of the mothers of a student told us how her daughter trembled in the evening when she thought of school. In the teacher conference, the background of the teacher was discussed.

Besides a teachers background, the fantasies present when entering the teaching profession are looked at. Why did a teacher choose teaching? What are the motives? With younger teachers it is often the case that a fantasy of the "pure" child lies behind their decision, and they orient themselves after an idealized image of the child. They view the child's world as unspoiled. According to this fantasy, the children have no Shadow but strive to be good. If the children are bad tempered, aggressive, or mean, the teacher holds the parents, the environment or society responsible. Violence is externalized in this fantasy. Ultimately these teachers project the divine child onto their students. They expect the children to be the carriers of hope for our society, and that they will change the world. Meanwhile, the children's Shadow is overlooked. If a girl regularly torments her desk mate, spits in his face, and cuts the back of his hand with scissors, a limitless disappointment spreads. If the children do not behave according to the projected purity, these teachers start to internally turn away from them and are disappointed because children are not better humans than we are.

Another common teaching fantasy is the hope of extending childhood. Sometimes people become teachers to turn to children out of fear of the adult world and of having to prove themselves in society. These teachers expect children to protect them from the adult world. They seek work with children because they feel politics and business is dirty and brutal. Instead of participating in this horrible world, they seek out their meaningful work with the future generation. The problem with this fantasy is that there is no room for violence and aggression. If a student is thrown down the stairs, or if weapons appear in the classroom, these teachers become insecure and are upset. The evil, adult world is breaking into their world of children. They are often almost paralyzed since now they have to face the existential challenges of society.

Another subject of the teacher conference is the history of the class. This is the events and incidents that are regarded as important by the teacher and the class. Each class has its own biography. The class's reputation belongs to this story. Here classes with frequent changes of teachers often have the reputation of "taking out teachers." Such a reputation influences a teacher's expectations when taking over a class.

In one class the teacher decided, from the start, to make his terms known directly and clearly. He believed he had to get control of his class by making tough demands. The students rebelled and started to cut classes. In the framework of a self-fulfilling prophecy, the class behaved according to the teacher's expectations. It became clear during the teacher conference that the teacher based his teaching methods on the past history and reputation of the class and not on his impression.

Of course the discussion of individual students belongs to the teacher conference. The crisis intervention can only begin if a precise image of the class has been sketched beforehand. Who are the shy children? Who is well behaved, and who is difficult? The behavior of individual students is viewed from the teacher's perspective.

Here it is important that the teacher can give free range to negative feelings and fantasies. If a student is irritating it may be mentioned in the context of this conference. The goal of the teacher conference is not an objective analysis, but to make conscious the teacher's own personal emotions towards the students.

Furthermore the teaching fantasies and ideals should be talked about in the teacher conference. How does the teacher want to teach? Does the teacher want a group orientated class? Does the teacher imagine mingling with the class or standing in the front? Many teachers identify with a particular teacher model. In their education teachers hear of a style that they want to imitate in the classroom. Unfortunately these teaching styles are often not easy to copy. A group lesson turns into chaos, and as a result of that lesson, only a third of the students have their homework done by the end of the week. This difference between practice and ideal can be painful for the teacher.

Reflection on one's teaching style is important because many teachers start out with the idea that there exists an ideal teaching style. They look for salvation in their didactic style and hope, when confronted with problems, for an even better teaching trick to solve problems. Their attention focuses on the technical, and they believe that the success of the lesson mainly depends on the teaching. They think, "There must be a didactic that can get the class enthusiastic!"

This belief is based on the notion that there actually is such a thing as a class. A class is viewed as an independent thing, and the lesson orients itself on the fiction of "a class." A comparison between the different classes quickly shows that a class *per se* does not exist. The teacher always stands in front of a *specific* group of students; classes differ greatly from one to another. In a class it is a question of grasping the particularities of *this* specific class. Is it a question of an introverted, dynamic, driven or demanding class? What does its profile look like? There is only the *individual* class, the class *per se* is a fiction. It is therefore not possible to talk about the best teaching style without keeping the particular class in mind. What is good for one class fails in another. The didactic style is to be developed in the interaction with the given class. While one class is in need of a lot of lecturing, so that the students can tune into the group through the teacher, another needs individualized teaching. It is important for the teacher to find out which style suits the class and to develop this according to preferences and possibilities. For new teachers, this is a long process. Unfortunately, a certain didactic-pedagogic system is taught in the schools of education. Which, during their education, the becoming teachers are all enthusiastic (excited). A class's individuality is thereby rarely given adequate consideration. In practice, young teachers often suffer disasters because they are fix onto a certain teaching style, yet they have not studied the profile of the class. In the first couple of weeks a teacher should focus on this subject and not begin with well prepared lectures. In order to find a psychological diagnosis of the class, the teacher should not meet the class with a lot of preconceived notions, but with a curious look that tries to recognize the complexes, resources, Shadow aspects and potentials of this group of students.

In conference with the teacher, the Shadow of the teaching profession is discussed. Do you suffer from burn out? Have you become bitter? With older teachers it often shows through their feeling of not connecting with the new generation. They become aware that they can no longer appear as dynamic young teachers and start to doubt themselves. With these teachers, violence and aggression in class triggers a great personal crisis. Do I still have enough energy? Am I already passé? These teachers count the years until their retirement.

In our crisis interventions we have shown that lacking a connection to the class is often only the surface problem. Teachers experience the feeling of burn-out while in fact they only had the bad luck of having a difficult class assigned to them. Previously they had three problem free classes. They then believe they are burned-out and do not recognize that the present class is just more difficult to teach than the previous one.

The reproaches of the students, of course, belong to the Shadow aspects of the teaching profession. During work with the class, the crisis intervention team hears criticism of the teacher. These accusations are brought up by the head of the crisis intervention team during the teacher conference. The teacher is confronted with the opinion of the students. "The students accuse you of being in a bad mood every morning! The students say you are not able to handle the difficult children!" It is important that these uncomfortable, often embarrassing, and wounding accusations not be avoided. One class noticed that the teacher pretended to have a boyfriend. The children sensed she was lying to them. Consequently they wrote a letter in which they said the teacher was a lesbian and falsely accused her of making sexual passes to the girls. These accusations of the class hurt the teacher deeply. Therefore the subject of sexuality in the classroom had to be taken on during the teacher conference.

Before the teacher conference begins with the leader of the crisis intervention team, the dialogue format is agreed upon. The head of the crisis intervention team plays the devil's advocate, consciously focusing on the uncomfortable Shadow. The leader tries to, in this way, break taboos with the intention of strengthening the teacher by allowing for weaknesses to be processed. It is not the intention of the leader to get down on the teacher's case or to be hyper-critical, but to bring to light the repressed subjects that the teacher wants to avoid. What consequences should be drawn is left up to the teacher. The leader of the crisis intervention team does not believe the criticism to be objective truth, but this criticism is to act as a catalyst, a spur, for the teacher's work. The teacher decides what conclusions to draw from it. If this form of working together is explained and agreed upon in advance, it is easier for the teacher to stand criticism, and use it in a positive way.

The duration's of the teacher conferences vary. As a rule there will be three to four sessions. It is important that the conferences are held on neutral grounds. Most often these are held in the offices of the school psychologists or guidance counselors .

The parents' evening

An integral part of every crisis intervention is the parents cooperation. A crisis intervention only has a chance at success if the parents support the work of the teachers and psychologists both emotionally and concretely. The limiting of violence in school is only possible when there is a mutual will. If the parents boycott the efforts of the psychologist, and if they mock the *psycho-games* that are to take place, this attitude is transferred onto the students. They become skeptical and do not believe in its possible success.

To get the parent's support is not easy. The suffering of their own child does not go by them without leaving its marks. Often there remains a feeling of bitterness or a desire for revenge. The situation is most difficult for parents whose children are considered problems. Over and over again they have to hear about their son's or daughter's misdeeds. As a rule, parents of so called "problems" reject the attacks on their sons or daughters. They say, "The class is only looking for a scapegoat! It is not my son's fault, the other children are simply teasing him and making him get mad. He's emotional."

After incidents in schools occur, parents develop their own versions of what happened and believe to know their causes. Therefore they are hardly willing to have the connections explained to them by psychologists. They expect the psychologist to fix the class according to their notions. It is the goal of the parents' night to break down a possible defensive wall and win the parent's cooperation. from the start the underlying model of the crisis intervention is explained to them. We explain that violence and aggression are viewed as a group phenomenon and that we do not intend to pick out the guilty. We treat the class as a whole. We want to mobilize the positive group aspects of the class so that the class can learn how to prevent violent outbursts. From the beginning it should be pointed out to the parents that it is not a question of giving therapy to their sons or daughters, but that the entire class should be strengthened.

Of course this picture is one sided. Every teacher knows that problematic children can poison the atmosphere in a class. However the crisis intervention does not focus on these children but focuses on the class's possibilities. It focuses on the group, knowing that the behavior of a difficult child cannot be changed through a brief intervention. The goal therefore is to change the difficult children's surroundings to such a degree that they no longer can get their way in class. A positive spirit in the class prevents violence and aggression from taking over.

This group psychological stance gives the parents the possibility to participate without the fear of their son or daughter being stigmatized and pathologized by psychologists. No one carries the blame and no one has to be held accountable. Instead it is posited that the mechanism of the group dynamics has led the children to violence. Even if the individual child behaves well, and is nice, accessible, and peaceful at home, it is possible that the same child can be seized by a group dynamic at school which results in violent acts. Also the known problem children are often victims of a negative dynamic within the class, for example, Beno was a child who was considered a "nasty student" by the entire village. In the crisis intervention, we found out that the class liked to keep him in this role so that they could settle quarrels through him.

In writing, the teacher invites the parents one or two weeks in advance to parents' night. It is important that as many parents as possible show up. If the teacher is aware of parents who do not want to come, it helps if they are called up beforehand and told the meaning of the evening, making it clear to them that their presence is required. With foreign parents it is recommended that some one contacts them who speaks their language. Before the parents' night, the impression has to be made that something significant is happening. The overall atmosphere should change. Something is going to be done against violence now. Together, we can and will confront violence.

On the invitation the subject, "violence and aggression in the class," is announced so the parents know what will be talked about. On the invitation the names of the members of the crisis intervention team is listed. It is important that the crisis intervention remains the sole subject of the evening. This is because, with other subjects under discussion, there is the danger of sliding into more harmless subjects when the class incidents are supposed to be talked about.

The greeting of the parents is done by the teacher. The teacher mentions that *he* or *she* called in the crisis intervention team and that he or she is also willing to work to understand his or her part in the violence. The teacher explains that he or she will not be spared during the intervention and that his or her teaching style will be examined. The teacher verbally supports the intervention and emphasizes that it correlates with his or her intentions.

In the beginning this point was not sufficiently considered by us. Bad experiences afterwards have taught us better. With one teacher we merely agreed that she would introduce the crisis intervention without telling her how. We were just a little surprised when she said the following words to the parents: ". . . and here I would like to introduce the psychological team of the Board of Education. They will execute a psychological experiment with the class!" It immediately became clear to us that this intervention would not succeed. The teacher at the last review refused participation and regarded us as the expert team that was supposed to make everything well without bothering her.

After the greeting from the teacher and possibly a member of the school board, the leader of the group explains the theory and procedures of the intervention. The leader introduces the theory described above, and also explains to the parents how work is going to be done with students on different afternoons, what our expectations are, and how the teacher will be included.

After the leader of the group is done speaking, the parents have the opportunity to give their views on the incidents and climate of the school. They should be able to express their anger, desperation, and expectations. While this may easily occur on regular parents' nights, it might happen that the parents hide their feelings and thoughts; the recent incidents are too painful. We have experienced a complete silence when we challenge the parents to bring up their concerns. No one dared say anything out of fear that it could effect their daughter or son. The next few days, the phone would then not stop ringing. Mothers and fathers phoned in order to inform us about the *real* conditions in the class *after* the evening.

So the evening has to be held in a way that parents can overcome their inhibitions and express themselves freely. Psychological exercises can help dismantle inner barriers and fears. One possibility is role diagnosis. After the team leader's explanations of the meaning of the group in itself, different roles within the group are briefly introduced: the mediator, the outsider, the tough, and the hanger on. The parents are asked to remember the days when they were in the same grade as their daughter or son and to reflect which of the mentioned roles they then played. On a small label they write the role that they chose and stick it onto their shirt or sweater. Now the parents are divided into groups. It is important that the groups are made up of people carrying different roles and that couples are not in the same group. In these subgroups, they should exchange their personal experiences as students in equivalent classes; "This is how it was when I went to fifth grade." This way parents automatically move into a discussion about the class of their child. The detour through childhood serves as a method to reduce personal fears. And the parents mix their own experiences with that of their children.

The goal of the discussion with the parents is to let the know how we work. Also the leader of the crisis intervention team is informed about the parents' concerns and get to hear what is bothering them. This would include incidents on the way to school, in the community, during free time, or on the playground.

On one parents' night, it became apparent that a group of students would regularly wait for the girls going to school and launch kiss attacks. The boys would throw themselves on a girl and cover her face with kisses. On a different parents' night, we learned that at home children were accusing friends of egging them on to be violent. So the fault was always blamed on someone else.

Often the parents have the teacher in their sights. They criticize the teacher's didactic style, or they demand that more detentions be given, or more group instruction, or that more drastic action has to be taken. In one crisis intervention, the complaints were that the teacher did not talk to the parents. The parents had the impression that the teacher was barricading himself and was emotionally not available to them. The teacher however had the feeling that the parents were not at all interested in being involved.

At the end of these discussions, there is usually a consensus that finally something has to be done. The violence has to stop. The demands may sometimes be put directly, as an ultimatum, to the teacher or to the crisis intervention team. "Why are you only here now? What are you planning to do?"

The head of the crisis intervention team has to return the ball. The leader has to emphasize that the work with the class and teacher can only begin with the parents' active support. The parents have to be in agreement with the crisis intervention and help carry it. Only in that way can and will we, as psychologists, begin with the work. The distinct support of the parents is important because otherwise the feeling, "If it does not help, it cannot hurt!" will spread around. The parents will then take a consumer attitude demanding the psychologists solve the problem: "The experts should handle the violence!" The head of the crisis intervention team has to anticipate this and emphasize that violence and aggression have to be tackled together with them. Without the parents' support, there can be no crisis intervention, and the crisis intervention team will draw back. The parents are given a choice: either be actively supportive or the intervention will be ended. Participation in the crisis intervention means that parents at home talk with their children about violence and aggression in daily life. They should not force children to give away secrets, but convey the feeling that now, something is going to be done. It is important that they and their children become sensitive to the subject of violence. Parents should not only talk about violence but also emphasize the possibilities of the crisis intervention.

Support also means that members of the crisis intervention team are informed about violent incidents. The parents should call the psychologist or teacher if they notice anything with their son or daughter, and if they have information that could help the crisis intervention team.

Through these procedures an expectant attitude should be created. Parents and children should be awakening with the feeling that now things are going to get better, and this should be created almost like a *self-fulfilling prophecy*. They must believe that it actually is possible to do something about violence. The paralysis that often occurs after a violent incident has to be overcome. Children should experience the crisis intervention as a break in their regular school day.

Most of the time all parents approve. It can happen that one or two parents remain skeptical. It is then left up to the crisis intervention team to decide whether to go ahead with the work or not. Afterwards we have seen that a child of skeptical parents reacted to their attitude and created larger problems. The child found the "psycho games" stupid or refused to take part in the work.

School visits

In order to plan the concrete work and begin with the actual crisis intervention, the crisis intervention team needs information about the school and its community. They need a personal impression of the class. For this purpose a member of the team visits one or several classes as well as the teachers' lounge. The playground is also briefly observed.

First of all it is important to gain a general impression of the school. How are the students received? Does the school seem inviting or unfriendly? In a school in Bern the school's rules were clearly written over the entrance. So when the children arrived at school in the morning, the first thing they were reminded was that they are not allowed to be inside the school building too early, that chewing gum is prohibited, that they have to be at their desk by the second bell etc. Meanwhile in another school building, the hallways are partially decorated by the students, yet another has busts of important men everywhere. Does a child feel comfortable in such hallways?

Each member of the crisis intervention team also gets an impression of the classroom's interior. What does the space encourage one to do? Are always three desks put together so that the students face each other or has the classic desk arrangement been chosen? Does the interior of the classroom encourage working groups or lecturing?

One classroom impressed us with its coziness. The teacher had lugged a couch from home and created a cozy corner behind the desks. One student at a time was allowed to relax there. With this living room atmosphere the teacher hoped to curb the violent incidents. The class clearly did improve. After summer vacation, she realized to her horror that the couch and chairs she had brought in had been removed. The janitor in agreement with the school administrators had thrown out these "school alien" objects.

Besides the classroom's decor, the visiting team leader should also take a look at the work of the class. This is done not to judge the achievements of the students, but to get an insight into the life of the class. The team leader tries to see something about the atmosphere in the class.

In one class it was noticed that, when assigned a paper with a choice of subject, over half of the class chose war, fights, or aggression as their topic. In their essays the students had cars and people's heads exploding. Students that otherwise were well behaved, produced horrible images in their papers. For the team leader this was a sign of the class's attempt at engaging the Shadow. He regarded it as an appeal from the children to help them deal with the horrible aspects of life.

Besides essays, drawings are also revealing. How do students represent themselves? What forms do they give themselves? In the drawings of another class it was noticed that many children walled themselves in. One student drew herself on the first floor of a house, another stood on top of a mountain surrounded by a forest, while a third student was in a tower without stairs. These children felt defensive.

Of course the team leader also visits a class, usually at a time and a subject where students work independently. The team leader looks for the class's group dynamic patterns. Can class leaders be recognized? Are there any subgroups? Is there tension? The team leader tries to look at the class based information from the teacher conferences. A picture should be formed from the quality of the relationship among students, the distribution of power, and style of communication.

In one class it was seen that students kept on teasing each other. When walking by they would briefly stick out their tongues, break a pencil, or whisper an obscene word. Many children let themselves be provoked by this and teased back. The little provocations became the norm of communication.

Besides the behavior of the class, the member of the crisis intervention team observes the teacher's teaching style. How is the class welcomed? How does the teacher talk to the class? Is the teacher in control of the students? Does the teacher radiate a certain optimism or depression? Here there are great differences. While there are teachers who start the week with the words, "Open your math books to page 40," others first sing a song with the class or tell a story. How the teacher responds to student questions is also part of the teaching style. A girl in third grade had injured herself on her wrist. She wore a colorful bandage and felt a bit sorry for herself sitting at her desk. When the teacher saw the bandage, she said rudely, "This colored stuff here, remove it right away!"

Visiting the teachers' room is also part of the school visit. Together with a teacher the crisis intervention team briefly enters the teachers' room. Also here the team tries to acquire some impressions. How do the teachers talk with each other? What do they talk about? How is the teacher, who called for the crisis intervention, being received? How is the room decorated? Here, also, there are great differences. Some teachers' rooms give the impression that there is a culture of lively discussion, where expressing concerns and angers is easy. In others there is a more reserved atmosphere. In the latter it is difficult to talk about personal problems. Anger is swallowed, it is quiet and talk concerns the up-coming holidays. Problems in the classroom are not spoken about, only possibly about certain difficult children. In such rooms parents are talked about snobbishly, but teacher behavior is not reflected on. The visit to the teachers' room gives an indication of the school culture.

During this visit the psychologist also casts an eye on the structure of the school complex. What hallway do the children take to go to gym? Where do they park their bicycles? How is the play ground designed? The crisis intervention team needs this information to be able to understand the concerns and descriptions of the class. Violence can be encouraged by structural inadequacies. In one school building it turned out that students arriving on bicycles had to use the same entrance as the students on foot. It created a crowded entrance. Most of the fights, threats and attacks happened in this bottle neck because the students on the bikes threatened the walkers.

The information collected by the member of the crisis intervention team during the visit subsequently serves as the basis for the planning of the work to be done with the class. These solid procedures are used to address the problem situation of the class and school.

Work with the class: the mythodrama

The next point is the work with the class. Three psychologists work with the entire class for three to four afternoons. This actual crisis intervention is carried out by one leader and two co-leaders, mostly advanced psychology students who have experience in group psychotherapy.

The class has to assemble in front of the gym. It knows that it will now, on several afternoons over three to four weeks, work together with the psychologists. The class is informed by the teacher and parents that the psychologists have come to them because of the violence in the school or in the class. They know that something is going to happen, that something should change. As a rule the students are very excited. They have great expectations. "What are they going to do with us?" This atmosphere is deliberately created so the students have the feeling that something important is about to happen. They are engaged and ready to work.

It is important how the crisis intervention team presents itself to the class. The team is not allowed to show any signs of ambivalence, shyness or insecurity on their initial contact. They appear as authoritative group leaders. When they near the gym, they avoid eye contact. Without taking up contact with the children directly, they tell them to assemble in the gym. The team has to make it clear that now they are in charge. The reason for this is that in many classes the leaders are the first who dare approach the crisis intervention team. On the first encounter they want to demonstrate to their friends that they are not afraid of these psychologists. Boldly they extend their hand and introduce themselves. If a crisis intervention member accepts this greeting, unknowingly this acceptance will strengthen the class leader's position and the old power will persists The crisis intervention team has to overthrow this old system so that more cooperative children get a chance at gaining acceptance. The purpose of making an appearance as the authoritative leader of a group is to trigger a new dynamic in the class. The children notice that the leader of the class cannot always get his or her way, and that he or she is not regarded as the big boss by the crisis intervention team. For the crisis intervention team the act as head leader of the gang leader group is often not easy. Since the team members are interested in individual children and actually are looking for contact, they have to change emotionally and, as actors would say, give themselves up to the role.

We pretend to be the leaders of a tough group although we of course know that it is all a bluff.

Once the class is assembled in the gym, the members of the crisis intervention team introduce themselves. Then the problem is mentioned by name. "We are here because there is violence in your class. You cannot handle the tensions and you are fighting." If the violent incidents are concentrated in the class, the class is addressed negatively by the leaders of the team. They inform the class of what a bad reputation they have, that they have messed up, and their behavior is unacceptable. This serves the to instigate counter forces within the class: "We are much better than this reputation!"

Furthermore the goal of the crisis intervention program is explained to the class. We say, "We want things to be better. The threats and violence has to decrease." The intervention team tells the children their expectations, which are that after the fourth afternoon of the intervention, they will be able to regulate the problem of violence themselves.

The teacher stays away from these afternoons. The teacher is not allowed to be present, because otherwise the class will begin adjusting themselves to the teacher. They will either try to provoke, anger or empathize with the teacher. The students will speak less of their fears and the incidents in the school if the teacher is present. Because the crisis intervention people are unknown figures, it is easier for the children to speak openly. The children have to know that the crisis intervention team specializes in problems in schools and is knowledgeable when it comes to the subject of violence and aggression.

We have observed how children sense exactly where they can tell something. On a school trip two boys dragged another student behind a house. They ordered him to take off his pants and wanted to shove a little stick up his anus—a terrible experience for the harassed boy. Following this the three of them returned to class. The abused boy did not mention anything to his teacher. Two weeks later he talked to a social worker on the school ground who was conducting an information week on the subject of violence. This social worker now told about the incident that happened in the trip. Later on this boy said, "I could tell the social worker because he knows what violence is. Besides it is his job to take us seriously."

After the welcome, the crisis intervention team does some warm up exercises with the class. We try to heighten the social perception of the class and help it have a group experience. Depending on the age of the students, different exercises are carried out.

A famous exercise is to try to communicate with one's hands. Two students face each other. They receive the instructions to imagine a strong emotion like rage, jealousy, fear, happiness, delight etc. Next they have to hold their hands half way up. With the palms of their hands facing outwards, through hand contact, they now have to communicate these emotions to their partner. Talking is not allowed. The communicating is limited to the touching of the hands only. The aim of this exercise is to heighten the sensibility for nonverbal communication. In other exercises the children should notice changes in their fellow students' clothing, or what can be expressed with their facial expressions. The main emphasis of the warm up exercises is in the communication in the class. The students communicate through verbal, visual and tactile signals with each other. They have to focus their attention on others.

With younger children we often apply fantasy and transformation games. They run around in the gym as an animal of their choice; roar like lions or jump like frogs. Maybe they are encouraged by the team leader to try out different ways of walking or to greet each other in different ways. With such exercises the group experience is foremost.

The actual mythodrama follows these tuning up exercises. The team asks the children to choose a spot on the gym floor to lie down on and try to calm down. Now the team applies relaxing techniques so that the children be peaceful. Contrary to adults, children need concrete images. "You are lying in a meadow.[1] Feel the grass between your fingers and feel how your arms are getting heavier and heavier." A description of a concrete scene is easier for the children to relax. "You see a long mountain path in front of you. Slowly you are climbing it. Now you have reached the peak and feel exhausted."[2] When the children are relaxed, they are ready to hear a story and visualize it. The next five to ten minutes the crisis intervention leader tells a story, a fairytale or a myth. The story is told orally. If the team leader reads from a book, it separates him from the children. As a story teller he concentrates on the children's group, tries to be impartial to their feelings and stay on the same level. The story serves as a medium through which the team leader enters into contact with the children. Like a shaman the leader tries to sense the feelings in the room and make intuitive adaptations. The process that takes place between the team leader and the students is important. The story is merely a medium for what will happen during the session. Most of the time the story is accompanied by

---

[1] Translator's note: Swiss children are not afraid of bugs or things in the grass as much as are other children in suburban or urban cultures.
[2] Translator's note: Swiss children are not afraid to hike up high mountains.

music. The music may, however, not have a clear motive or recognizable melodies, because it could distract the children.

In myths or fairytales children are confronted with problems, difficulties and challenges that they have in the class. The stories are chosen from that perspective. Yet the stories have to also present a mental challenge. It should not be a well rounded, moralizing story with a clear message, but a story that leaves the children perplexed: a man suddenly turns into a spider or a boy is challenged with a seemingly impossible mission. The stories are supposed to make the children curious and stimulate their thinking. Furthermore it is important that the stories have an archetypal style to them and describe situations and problems that exist in our collective psyche as *ur*-patterns; for example the overcoming of fear, confrontation with the terrifying, abuse, fear of the powerful, cowardliness, etc. The story should pose a psychological challenge that the child has to face in school. Here is a good example of a story I often use. It is called *Alexander's Travels*, and it is from a letter Alexander the Great ostensibly wrote to his mother Olympia.

> After I conquered king Darius, I started out and conquered many kingdoms all the way to distant Persia, over which Darius had ruled. From there I wanted to march on into the depth of the desert in the direction of the Big Dipper. We came to a region full of deep canyons; tight and rough were the roads on which we had to continue for eight long days. When we had left this desolate region behind us, we arrived at an even dimmer place. In a great forest we found trees that carried a foreign and rare fruit; apples the seize of pumpkins were hanging on them. In this forest lived humans who were twenty four yards tall and had necks of a length of one and a half yards. Their hands

and arms were like sharp saws. Immediately they fell upon our army. I gave the order to capture one of them. They fled when we threw ourselves on them with shouts and trumpet sounds,. Many of these strange beings we slew, yet they had killed even more of my men.

We then reached a country where wild giants lived that looked like lions. Also they wildly fell upon us and killed many of my men. Out of fear that they could conquer us, I had the forest set on fire. When these giant men saw the fire, they fled.

The next day I decided to explore their caves. There we met wild animals that were tied to the entrance of the cave. They looked like lions and each had three eyes. We also saw fleas jumping around there that were as large as frogs. From there we marched back and reached a place with a bubbling spring. There I made camp and stayed for two months.

From there we reached the land of the apple eaters. There we saw a man whose body was completely covered with fur. We were horrified by the monster, and I ordered him captured. He was brought to us, and without fear he looked at us a prisoner. I then let a naked woman be brought to him. He however grabbed her and started to eat her. When the soldiers ran to pull the woman away from him, he started to roar. This was heard by his friends and about one thousand men who looked like him emerged from the swamps and fell upon us. I however had the swamp plants set on fire and immediately they fled. In the chase we captured three of them. They refused to eat and so they died one week later. They did not have a human appearance, did not speak but barked like dogs.

We went on and came to a river where I set up camp. In the river there were trees that started growing at sunrise. In the afternoon they became smaller again until they again finally disappeared. They had a wonderful smell and their resin was like Persian myrrh. When I gave the order to fell the trees and soak their resin with sponges, the collectors were whipped by invisible beings. We heard the cracking of the whip and saw the marks on their backs. And an invisible voice suddenly arose and forbade us to cut the trees and collect the resin. "If you continue to cut the trees and collect the resin," the voice said, "the whole army will loose its voice and become mute." Overcome with fear, I called back my men and stopped cutting the trees.

In the same river we also discovered black stones. When one touched these, one turned as black as they. Many snakes and fish moved about in this river. These could not be cooked in hot water but were already tender in cool spring water. Also birds lived there who looked similar to ours, if one touched them however, they would spit fire. The following day we went about. Ten days we went along without seeing the light of the sun. Many strange animals crossed our way, some with six feet, with three or five eyes, monsters who were ten yards long. Then we came to a sand desert where animals twenty yards long lived. They looked like our wild donkeys and every animal had six eyes; they could however only see with two. They were tame and did not attack us, and so my men slew many of them with their bows.

We then came to a place where people without heads lived. They were hairy and dressed in skins. They caught fish on the seashore and brought them to us. There we also saw large seals crawling around on land. Although my friends advised me to turn back, I did not want to return because I wanted to see the ends of the world.

> We continued the march all the way to the ocean.
> We did not see anything anymore, no birds or mam-
> mals. For ten days there was darkness.[3]

Not always is the story told to the end. Often we in-
terrupt it in the middle, asking the children to make up
their own endings. Such a story, told by heart, and modi-
fied most of the time, is supposed to help children become aware of their feelings. It may however not reflect
the problem of the class too directly. If the children become aware of the intentions behind the story, they reject
it. They think, "it is obvious these psychologists want to
talk to us about our fighting." The story should cause
astonishment and prepare the emotional ground later
necessary for the group work. It is therefore not a question of instructive stories, but having stories to warm up
their imagination.

While stories and myths are used for younger children, it is also recommended to tell true stories to older
children. One class was told about the airplane crash in
the Andes mountains where a rugby team had to eat their
dead teammates in order to survive. Another class was
told about an incident after the Second World War where
a former German soldier lived for twenty years next to a
presumed dead loved one. While the children are listening to the story they concentrate with closed eyes on internal images and feelings.

The stories that we tell the children have to have an
eerie to horrible quality. They describe horrible scenes
where people are beheaded, burned, quartered, or chased
by monsters. We tell children about the horrors of the
world. The following ideas are behind this procedure.

---

[3] Erich Ackermann, *Fairytales from Antiquity* (Frankfurt: Fischer,
1989), 102-108.

We have noticed that children do not like to listen to stories with happy endings. They become restless and their minds begin to drift. Also stories with moral messages are unfavorable; internally resistance starts to arise. The reason for this behavior lies in the principle of the tension of opposites of the human psyche. This idea, borrowed from the alchemical writings of C. G. Jung, states that processes of the soul play themselves out through a tension of opposites. If one side is over emphasized, the attraction of the opposite pole rises. Relating this to the stories, it means that the opposite effects are constellated in the children. When we tell them about good deeds maybe they consciously agree with the message. Internally however resistance arises. Particularly difficult, problem classes react allergically to "goody-goody-stories." Yet if they get to hear stories that contain horror and terror, paradoxically the children's good sides are constellated. The terrifying has found its place in the story so that the children can now be peaceful and relieved of the burden of having to produce their horrible sides.

It is important that the children develop their own terrifying images and are not directly confronted with horrible images for example in brutal videos. With fantasy images, the present condition of the particular student is imagined. They hear of horror, fantasize, and in this way have an opportunity grapple with their fears. By bringing the terrible into the school, children are relieved of acting it out themselves.

After listening to the story, the children are allowed to open their eyes, and the next phase begins which is the working through of emotions and feeling that the children have experienced. This working through can happen in different ways. One possibility is to hand each child colored paper and pens to draw a picture of the story. Or the class can be divided into groups to decide on an ending to the story and perform it for each another. Further possibilities are: painting a picture together, doing a musical performance, improvised theater, etc. The important thing is that the emotions and personal experiences that come up during the telling of the story find a pictorial or staged portrayal. The students are not allowed to be left alone with the fears that might have emerged.

In one class a boy started to remember an experience he had had on the playground. He had been forced to kiss his friends sneakers. This incident humiliated the boy deeply. The team leader had to give the boy the opportunity to describe his experience in a subgroup. It was a great relief for this boy to be able to talk about the humiliation, which occurred after the team leader's story had dissolved the emotional blockade.

Often a drawing shows indications of what preoccupies the children. If a student draws himself as hanged or crosses himself out with thick black lines, these are signs of alarm. Maybe the child is suffering, feels threatened, and frightened. It is the job of the team leader to take a close look at these drawings and reflect on what the child's soul is expressing.

On the first and second afternoon of the crisis intervention, the children should have the opportunity to express themselves about the situation at school, individually or in small groups. It is recommended that, for a short while, the class be divided into subgroups. In these groups the children are more likely to have the courage to express what they think of the class or school. Often it is difficult for them to talk in front of everybody. The talk in the subgroups has to be encouraged by the crisis team members. The previously acted theater scenes or the drawings can serve as a starting point. "Why are you choosing so much red? What do all those weapons mean in your picture?" Through the picture you reach the children's concerns and fears. They tell how they are terrorized by classmates, or that they are exposed to threats, or often get angry themselves. They speak more freely since the story helped deflect their own private horrors.

An example of a Turkish girl was impressive. We were told by her teacher and classmates that she did not understand one word of German. She kept to herself yet was continually tormented by her classmates. Her school bag was taken away from her, children would lay in wait for her on her way home, and several times she was threatened sexually. The Turkish girl suffered quietly. During classes she was silent. So we were astounded when, during discussions in the subgroups, she suddenly started to speak. In broken German she told us how mean the class was to her. She was afraid and would prefer to go back home.

Through conversations with the students, it becomes apparent that children first externalize violence and aggression. During the first session children often describe how they are threatened by students from *other* classes. The mean sixth graders or the homeboys from outside their school are the problem. The students' statements and concerns often do not differ from those of the parents. Most children are also upset over the incidents and think that something has to be done. The blame however is put on others. Only after the second or third crisis intervention, do we, as a rule, succeed in getting the children to admit their part in the violence.

After the working through phase, there follows a round discussion. The team asks the children to sit in a circle on the floor in the framework of a class discussion about themselves and their class. The only terms that the team demand is that after this conversation, something has to change in the classroom or in the class, so there will be less violent incidents.

This discussion often proceeds sluggishly. The students are not always able to express themselves in front of the entire class. Cautiously they tell about the problems and possible solutions. They say things like, "We carry too many weapons, steal from and torment each other." The circle discussion is important because the children should express the concerns and fears that they brought up individually or in the subgroups in front of the large group. Through the circle discussion the feeling should be created that something has to be done together to make things better. Therefore the children are encouraged to develop ideas as a group on how to prevent further violence in from happening.

Often the initial suggestions are rather immature and express a certain helplessness. One student suggests that "We should just be nice with each other," or states "From now on everything will be different." Such statements do express good intentions but are soon forgotten. It is important that the children decide on a concrete change. One class finally agreed to create a corner with a mat where students fighting could withdraw. In another class the desks were rearranged. Instead of groups of four, they arranged all of the desks in straight rows. Another class introduced two signals; red meant that everyone was to concentrate on the lesson and not talk, and green meant whispering was allowed. Through these signs, the new seating order, or the mat in the classroom, the students were reminded of their intentions after the crisis intervention had taken place; the changes serve as a memory aide. The changes can also concern the behavior in the class. "What are we going to do when it comes to a fight? How are we going to react if a classmate is threatened? What are we going to do if weapons turn up?" The class agrees on how to proceed in such questions. In the case of weapons, the teacher is to be notified immediately. If brutal fights occur, intervene. Often through such agreements, children who otherwise are more reserved and problem free, feel challenged to get involved in the conflict resolution. In a sixth grade, it led to a subgroup of three girls and two boys looking taking charge of order. They announced that in the future they would intervene when a classmate was bothered by other students. The threat had an effect. There were hardly any more incidents in this class.

In the circle discussion, not only are concrete measures talked about, but also what should happen if the agreements are broken. The children have to agree on sanctions that can be established by the teacher. What should happen if a child talks although the red sign is up? How should the teacher react if a girl is threatened or if a boy's bicycle is vandalized? The initial suggestions of the students are often radical. They suggest the teacher slap the guilty child or pull it by the hair. It is the duty of the team leader to convince the children of civilized sanctions like work or being moved into another class for one or two hours, having the person's name mentioned on the loudspeaker, etc. According to our experience, most children demand that the teacher enforce the sanctions. They see the teacher not only as a nice friend or teaching guide, but also want the teacher to assume the duty as head of the class. Although they do not always convey this directly to the teacher, they want action when rules are broken.

The following day the class has to inform the teacher on the agreed upon measures. Independently, without being urged, they tell the teacher what measures they want to introduce. The students are aware of the fact that the teacher has a right to veto. The teacher decides whether or not the children's suggestions are suitable. Until now, no teacher has had to make use of the veto. The students chose measures they knew would be acceptable to the teacher.

With difficult classes it can be helpful if a member of the crisis intervention team is present in the classroom the morning after the intervention. Discreetly it helps the children to present the suggestion and make the changes. Besides concrete changes, the punishments that will be adopted if measures and resolutions are useless and violent behavior keeps on occurring, have to be discussed with the teacher.

The teacher comes to an oral agreement with the class which forms the basis for further cooperation. The children are now aware of what is going to happen if they break their agreements. They are know the punishments. Beforehand the team leader informs the teacher about the children's notions in terms of punishments so the teacher knows which ones the children prefer and will accept.

It is important that the cooperation between teacher and class is placed on a new foundation. The class, as well as the teacher, should have the feeling of a break; from now on everything will be different! The teacher might change a teaching style and introduce new principles while the students try to stick to their suggestions.

Naturally the concrete measures decided by the students do not get rid of the causes of violence and aggression. It would be naive to believe that with the help of a mat, violence in the classroom will disappear. It is not the concrete measures that count, but the change of mood that it induces. Through this concrete suggestion of change, the class has the feeling of doing something against violence themselves, and that strengthens the class's collective feeling of worth. It feels less at the mercy of violence but instead sees possibilities of overcoming it and bringing about something as a group. The concrete change serves as a sign that the class possesses counter forces that can be mobilized when incidents occur. Thanks to this change of mood, rituals can be developed to curb violent outbursts, which children will adhere to unconsciously when violence becomes a threat.

In the class that introduced the signals, violent incidents were reduced. Yet there would still be fights and beatings, though the disputes were less brutal. The children built up inhibitions. No longer did it happen that knives or clubs were used in fights. The children limited themselves to fists. Through the intervention, the class became aware that they previously had overstepped a line. The concrete change expressed the new social attitude of the class. Through them the children were continuously reminded that they could do something against violence themselves. The goal of the concrete measures is to cause changes in the social behavior and to introduce rituals against violence. These points cannot be established or planned in advance but have to be developed by the students. The concrete measures and discussions about punishments give the children the necessary impulse so they can find their way to a positive group behavior.

High school

In middle school, the crisis intervention team works with the class three to four weeks during one afternoon a week. A different approach is chosen with the high school. There the work with the class does not expand over one month, but usually a week is organized. The subject of violence and aggression is dealt with for three to four days. In high school the crisis intervention team presents itself as gang leaders, yet certain things are done differently than in the middle school. Stories no longer are necessary. The subject of violence and aggression is directly tackled. The students are more capable of self reflection because of their age. They have started to become interested in themselves, their identity, and role in the group. We therefore try address these capabilities and qualities during the crisis intervention. It is also apparent that teenagers are ready to reflect on a group's dynamics.

In one high school class, the focus was on creating a mural. The class was asked to sketch plans for a common mural. Different subgroups were formed that came up with suggestions. The subgroups were handed spray cans and were asked to make a sketch and then to interpret it.

The crisis intervention team had built in some traps. For instance one team received spray cans that had already dried out. Another was offered drinks while all the others went thirsty. With such disturbances we hoped to expose the class's way of dealing with conflicts. A member of the crisis intervention team had put up a video camera and filmed the class during their work. Afterwards the video was edited so that the significant scenes could be shown. The crisis intervention team chose those incidents that it found typical in terms of the class's dynamics.

On the second day it was explained to the class why and how in every group certain roles are formed. After the students were introduced to four to five different roles, we showed them the video and challenged them to identify their role in the class. At the second showing, they had to try to identify the roles of their classmates. This exercise helped the teenagers reflect on themselves and to realize that they were exposed to group dynamic processes. Once the question of what role they had in the class had been examined, we led them into the question of group dynamics.

After the crisis intervention, the team members urge the class to stick to their agreements. We then say good-bye to them, yet announce an upcoming visit in three to four months in order to see how the class is doing. It is important that the students know that the crisis intervention team will be back.

After completion of the initial phase of the work with the students, the leader of the crisis intervention or an assigned school psychologist, stays in touch with the teacher. In regular meetings the psychologist discusses the atmosphere of the class. The long term affect is what is important here. Are the children sticking to their agreements? Does the new teaching style have an effect? Often it is the efforts slacken after two or three weeks. If a class has calmed down, there is the danger that the teacher will throw the agreed upon arrangements out. They think, "Things are better, so why should I continue to threaten with punishments or keep the changes in the classroom?" Many teachers have the tendency to fall back on their old teaching style, because they believe that the problem is now solved. Unfortunately it has been seen that the old problems in the class promptly reappear. It is therefore important to support the teacher in this in-between phase, so the old mistakes do not creep back.

The same holds true for the class. Here it is a matter of perseverance. Often it is helpful if the crisis intervention leader talks to the class two to three times about the agreements made during the afternoons. In the teacher's absence, the class brings up concerns and wishes. They also tell the crisis intervention leader their worries. The leader reminds the class about its agreements.

The follow-up

After the in-between phase of three to four months, the group leaders meet with the class once more. On this last afternoon, there is a review, the current class situation is discussed, and resolutions for the future are made.

The program of this last afternoon differs from the previous ones. As a rule, no more mythodramas are acted out. Instead the students improvise some theater, paint or play together after the warm up exercises. The structure of the mythodrama—tuning in, relaxation, story, revision and the round talk—is consciously broken. The following afternoon a different emphasis is fixed. In this way it is made clear to the children that the crisis intervention is coming to an end. Through different kinds of programs, the expectation that the class as well is changed is voiced.

Although as a rule, the students participated in the first three to four afternoon programs, many classes reject the last intervention. They have had enough of the "psycho-games" and do not want to be considered a problem class any longer. This reaction is understandable and is brought on by the crisis intervention team. In this way, the class expresses that it rejects its negative reputation. It has developed a positive image and does not regard itself as the black sheep in the school. As a class it can settle fights and handle problems.

During the final intervention session, each student is asked whether the intervention helped them. In these interviews, or in front of a video camera, the students describe the incidents that have occurred over the past three to four month and talk about how they feel in school. As a rule, over half of these children have the impression that the school climate has improved thanks to the crisis intervention, and that the violent incidents have decreased. One quarter to one third of the students believe that they have not experienced any great changes. Frequently the children say there still are fights but they are less brutal.

The final evening with the parents

After the last crisis intervention the parents are invited to a closing evening. On that evening the crisis intervention leaders talk about their work and their impression of the class. They limit themselves to describing the group dynamics within the class without commenting on individual students. The crisis intervention team points out what circumstances encourage violence and how violence can be faced. From their subjective perspective, they describe their impression. Based on this picture of the class, the parents then are capable of talking with each other and can form plans.

In a high school class it became clear that the children kept on taking sides with bad students in the class. Out of the desire for a common challenge, the children backed the students whose behaviors were criticized by the teacher. When a teacher threatened a girl that he was not going to take her along for the class trip because she was regularly late for school and was caught stealing, her classmates were full of indignation. Between the teacher and the class a battle front was created. The class defined itself through the most difficult student. In working with the class however, it became clear that many students were annoyed by this girl's behavior. It bothered them that she played hooky for several days without any consequences. Furthermore it upset them that no one insisted she do her homework. The class had repeatedly identified itself with difficult students. The pattern was always the same. A student was caught violating a rule or committing an act of violence. The teachers or administrators tried to punish the act whereupon the class would immediately back the offender. This negative dynamic was broken through using crisis intervention. The students slowly began to pull away from the influence of these negative students and started to make their demands: we will support you going on the school trip as long as you disturb class no more.

On the closing evening, besides the crisis intervention leader's descriptions, the teacher presents the class's current situation. How did he or she experience the intervention? Has the atmosphere improved in the class? What pedagogic consequences has he or she, as a teacher, drawn from the work with the crisis intervention? What does the future look like?

The comments of the crisis intervention team and teacher can be complemented by a student made video. Through the film they tell their parents how they experienced the intervention. Often however the children refuse to allow the video, shot during the last crisis intervention, shown. They experience it as being to intimate. "What is said in therapy is not meant for outside!" a fifth grader brusquely replied to me when I asked her for her permission.

After the teacher's and crisis intervention leader's remarks, and after the movie, the parents have the opportunity to relate their impressions. Have they noticed any thing in their child? Also here the responses differ. Many parents claim in the aftermath that things were never that bad. The view changes as soon as there are no more serious incidents in school. The past is changed, the enraged outbursts, accusations and desperation of the first parents' nights are forgotten. When violence has disappeared as a common problem, the parents' willingness to engage the class's psychology decreases. They pull back as soon as they notice that their son or daughter is not suffering at school anymore.

Usually parents also report that their children feel better and confirm that violent incidents have decreased. At the end of the parents' night, the future cooperation between parents and teachers is discussed. The crisis intervention and the two parents' nights provide a basis for future cooperation.

Final thoughts

Crisis intervention with aggressive school classes distinguish themselves through five main points.

1. The work of the crisis intervention team aims at a class's resources. It wants to initiate a change in mood so that the class can find its solutions. It is a question of strengthening the students who produce a positive social attitude and have conflict resolving capabilities. This is done so that students with good social skills set the tone and not the difficult children.

2. It is important in the crisis intervention that all concerned parties actively participate: parents, students, school administrators, and teachers. If one of these parties is left out, the crisis intervention can fail. Only when all systems are taken into consideration, is there a prospect for success.

3. The focus is aimed at the entire class and not at individual students. Often, at the end of an intervention, it does turn out that this or that student does have particular problems, but the care of these students is no longer the duty of the crisis intervention team.

4. Through the mythodrama, the frightening stories and the circle discussions, the terrible in human existence is consciously brought into school. Only through

confrontation with our ugly sides can we hope that they will not control us.

5. Violence and aggression in school can only be overcome *with* the students and not *against* them. A crisis intervention seeks to help the children fortify themselves to give them the ability to take on the problems of violence and aggression.